ANCIENT EGYPTIAN HIEROGLYPHS
ILLUSTRATED

ANCIENT EGYPTIAN HIEROGLYPHS
ILLUSTRATED

A Formal Writing System Used in Ancient Egypt

Trevor Naylor

Amber Books Ltd
United House
North Road
London N7 9DP
United Kingdom
www.amberbooks.co.uk
Instagram: amberbooksltd
Facebook: amberbooks
Twitter: @amberbooks

ISBN: 978-1-83886-323-4

Design: Keren Harragan
Editorial: Michael Spilling
Copy Editing: Suzanne Arnold
Picture Research: Terry Forshaw

Printed and bound in China

TRADITIONAL CHINESE BOOKBINDING
This book has been produced using traditional Chinese bookbinding techniques,
using a method that was developed during the Ming Dynasty (1368–1644) and
remained in use until the adoption of Western binding techniques in the early
1900s. In traditional Chinese binding, single sheets of paper are printed on one
side only, and each sheet is folded in half, with the printed pages on the outside.
The book block is then sandwiched between two boards and sewn together
through punched holes close to the cut edges of the folded sheets.

Contents

Introduction

The 17th century German scholar and polymath, Athanasius Kircher, published some 40 important works in fields such as comparative religion, geology and medicine. He has recently been called 'the last Renaissance Man'. One of his greatest academic achievements was *Oedipus Aegyptiacus*, a massive, wide-ranging study of ancient Egypt and comparative religions. This work earned Kircher the sobriquet 'the founder of Egyptology'. Kircher said of hieroglyphs, 'this language hitherto unknown in Europe, in which there are as many pictures as letters, as many riddles as sounds, in short as many mazes to be escaped from as mountains to be climbed'. Little of his work with this alphabet proved to be accurate, but the field of Egyptology had been born. Kircher was also the earliest scholar to make an association between the Coptic language and ancient Egyptian, perhaps informed by his belief that these symbols were the language of Adam and Eve.

The rediscovery of hieroglyphic language truly began with the decipherment of the Rosetta Stone by Jean-François Champollion. Hieroglyphs continued to exert a fascination once Champollion had unlocked the door to their mysteries. Scholars, tourists, writers and Egyptophiles continued to be drawn to understanding the over 2000 symbols that 5000 years of civilization created.

The race had begun, to trace the whole story of Egypt's past through the millions of symbols covering buildings, objects, tombs, temples and papyrus. These were being discovered as European and American explorers came in droves to claim their place in archaeological history. Egyptomania followed, topped off by the finding of Tutankhamun's tomb, some 100 years ago.

The hieroglyph continued to fascinate, and its translation was recorded in key works of reference. The great scholar EA Wallis Budge created a staple volume for all Egyptologists with *An Egyptian Hieroglyphic Dictionary*. Another name of long-lasting significance was Alan Gardiner, who worked with Howard Carter to decipher inscriptions in the tomb of Tutankhamun.

Athanasius Kircher (1602–80)

His real gift to Egyptology, however, was a work on Middle Egyptian hieroglyphs and 'Gardiner's Sign List', a short guide that is as essential to those reading tomb walls today as when it was published in 1927.

What more, then, can be written on this enduringly captivating subject? This book gives an overview of a complex, multi-faceted language. It is designed to show a way into a subject that, when you are greeted with walls and objects covered in thousands of symbols, can appear as daunting as it is exciting.

Hieroglyphs tell stories of all aspects of life, from the powerful belief that gods were everywhere and needed to be pacified to reflections on the daily lives of hardworking people. These symbols also proclaimed that the pharaoh held power over man and nature to ensure a sense of stability in a land ruled by the vagaries of one river. Hieroglyphic amulets were another use of these symbols, the email of the day, with major events posted countrywide. Given the importance of this language to those who could read, Egypt's elite, the royal cartouches of rulers from Rameses to Cleopatra are also highlighted.

No journey of complex investigation can be successful without useful finds, or key discoveries as they are presented later. Some items, such as the Narmer Palette, and the Rosetta Stone, have transformed our knowledge of Egypt's full story. Hieroglyphs can also take us to the immortal worlds that obsessed those of 5000 years ago. The afterlife was the place all Egyptians wanted to be, because it would be perfect. Some of the many symbols that reflected that desire are discussed in this book.

Ancient Egyptians looked out at the stars in clear dark skies and sought to record these mortal and immortal worlds. This book explores the language they used to describe it, and allows me to explore a different world I have been fascinated by since childhood. I hope you enjoy this journey.

Trevor Naylor – March 2023

Narmer Palette

History of the Language

The relative stability of the ancient Egyptian civilization allowed
for a period of unparalleled and sustained development. Its
success left the modern world with a legacy of over 3000 years
of buildings, objects, art and knowledge, which continues to be
discovered and interpreted to this day. Surviving pictorial text
has been the key to unlocking the story of this civilization. The
development of ancient Egyptian language has been divided
into three main periods by those who have studied its evidence.
The first early writings, in what's referred to as Old Egyptian,
date to the period that ended in c. 2240 BC. This long period
of writing development had lasted almost 1000 years and was
mostly linked to recording royal and religious history, and
included much of the era known as the Old Kingdom.

The second period of language development, known as Middle
or Classical Egyptian, lasted until c. 1990 BC. The language had
by then achieved a sophisticated and consistent voice, which is
why this is often the period of hieroglyphs used for study. Middle
Egyptian was widely used, including for texts beyond the official
work and traditional funerary use of previously, providing a more
intimate understanding of ancient Egyptian life.

Middle Egyptian writing and its alphabet were in standard use
until approximately halfway through the New Kingdom era
(c. 1300 BC), after which Late Egyptian dominates. During this
time hieroglyphs are believed to have changed to more accurately
represent the spoken word of the era. There remained much
overlap between the various periods of Middle and Late Egyptian.
Throughout the millennia of this great civilization ancient
Egyptian remained the language of religion, administration and
daily life. The demise of this unique writing system and the end of
ancient Egypt owe much to each other's disappearance.

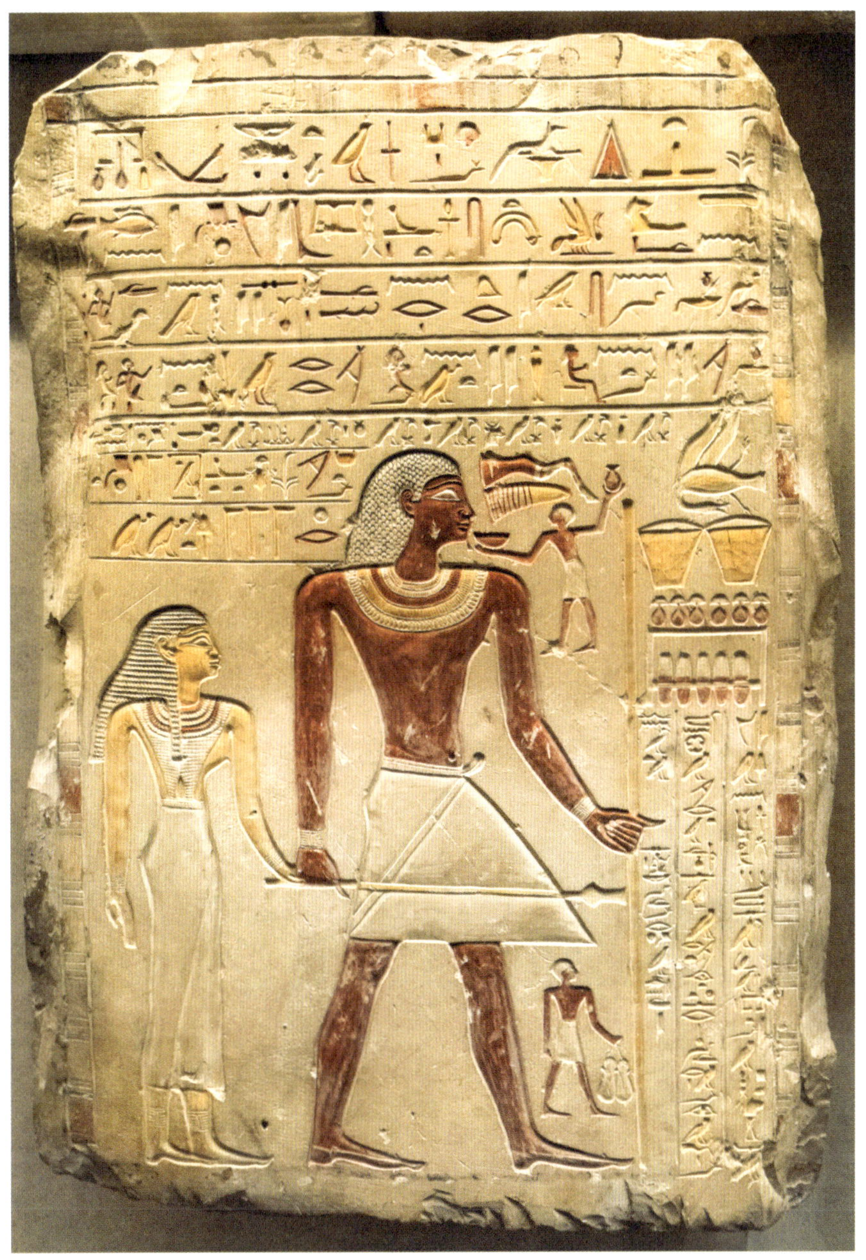

Funerary stela of Royal Sealer Indi and his wife Princess Hathor Mutmuti. Royal sealers were high-ranking treasury officials and oversaw the sealing of important documents (2150–2110 BC).

Scribe and Society

Hieroglyphs developed over many royal dynasties and represented an ever increasing sophistication in knowledge and religious beliefs. They also recorded ancient Egyptian civilization as it evolved a complex administration and religion. The control of language to reflect this evolving society fell to the scribes of ancient Egypt. Their work for the ruling class, pharaohs, priests, local administration and the military effectively ensured that control of writing and records put the scribes in the very upper layers of Egypt's power structure.

The need for scribes grew with Egypt's success. Those who learned to write were generally already in Egypt's upper echelons. The classes they attended to learn hieroglyphs took place in temples. It is thought that trainees learned these skills between the ages of 15 and 18. Being taught in a temple also underlined to ancient Egyptians the almost divine nature and power of the writing system. Once they were qualified, and had served their apprenticeship, graduates had a range of possibilities open to them. In a society broadly divided into religious, administrative, military and private business, the opportunities for those with writing skills were many and highly valued.

The words of some individual scribes can still be read today, and the status they achieved in life and beyond understood. Studying them is one way to understand the way the hieroglyphic language worked within society at the time, and how their legacies have opened up Egyptian life to the modern historian. One famous scribe was called Menna, whose colourful tomb in Thebes dates to the New Kingdom era. His highly decorated resting place suggests a successful career as scribe, which included the titles 'Scribe of the Lord of the

Two Lands' and 'The Eyes of the King in Every Place'. Menna oversaw other scribes who recorded such events as the annual yield of the fields and the prosecution of those who defaulted on payments to the state. The role of scribe held such status that wealthy men commissioned statues of themselves sitting in the traditional scribe form, crosslegged and writing, to enhance their own importance. 'The Seated Scribe' sculpture in the Louvre Museum, Paris, is one of the most famous representations of such figures. Dating from 2600 BC, it was discovered in Saqqara. He is shown here with the papyrus scroll across his knees, and the hand in its writing position, though the pen is missing. A pharaoh would commission a sculpture of their scribe for their tomb and this is believed to be the case here. It was obviously inconceivable for pharaohs to enter eternity without a scribe to serve them.

This Seated Scribe sculpture was discovered at Saqqara, site of the Step Pyramid and Serapeum. He holds a half-rolled papyrus. His hands, as scribe, are carefully detailed.

Hieroglyphic Alphabet

Egyptian script came into being some 4000 years before the
birth of Christ. By the time all of Egypt's temples were closed
at the command of Byzantine Emperor Theodosius I in
AD 391, the hieroglyphic script comprised over 2000 symbols.
Within these symbols, those decoding the story of ancient
Egypt identified 24 symbols that could be used phonetically,
as individual letters shown here, rather than as pictures
representing a whole concept or object.

The fact that this ancient language was written without vowels
presented serious issues for those attempting to read ancient
Egyptian aloud. There was little evidence of how the words of a
long-extinct language had been spoken in life. However, those
working from the Rosetta Stone had one invaluable starting
point – the echoes of ancient Egyptian speech that survived in
the Coptic language, which by then was written in the Greek
script. This allowed for modern vowels to be attached to certain
signs as their spoken sound only, rather than their written
form. This basic alphabet is in common educational use today,
introducing children, students, readers and tourists alike
to the thrill of this language and special civilization that
gave birth to it.

The pronunciation of the letters is a complex lesson in
practise, memory and good humour. Once these are mastered,
attempts should be made at biliteral signs, where an individual
hieroglyph represents two consonants. Single-sound and
double-sound symbols together allow the student to understand
much of the art they encounter when they visit Egypt or
collections of Egyptian art around the world.

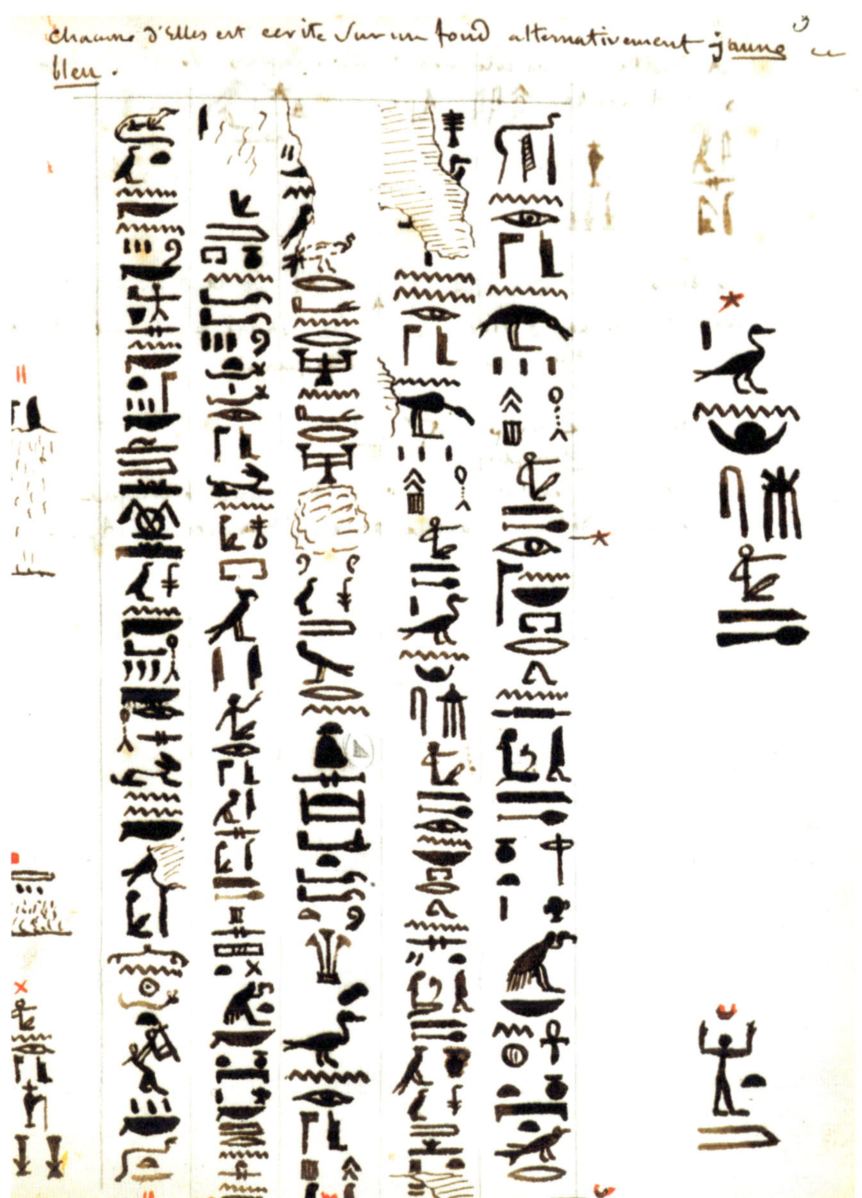

Hieroglyphic letters and symbols in the notebook of Jean-François Champollion,
translator of the Rosetta Stone.

Sign of the Times

Hieroglyphs drew their origins from the world around the river
Nile and the life and imagination of Egypt's rulers, scribes and
priests. As the ancient Egyptians' knowledge of the world and
the universe expanded, so did the number of logograms or
ideograms (used to illustrate actual objects, words or events),
phonograms (representing sounds) and determinatives (signs
used to clarify meanings of words). Over the length of ancient
Egyptian history, the hieroglyphic alphabet continued to expand
in numbers; however, the core of the written language
is centred on some 700 more commonly used symbols.

Hieroglyphs often cover a surface from floor to ceiling, or a
whole side of papyrus or an object. Interpreting them means
following certain rules, such as direction of reading. For
instance, sentences may be written from left to right, and from
right to left. The direction of reading is determined by the
direction the humans, animals, birds or gods are themselves
facing. Such symbols face towards the beginning of the
sentence. Hieroglyphs can also be written to read from top to
bottom, but not the reverse. Understanding the hieroglyphic
alphabet today remains a complex task for the beginner, with
a language that may be read in different directions and where
many hieroglyphs have more than one meaning. After the
deciphering of the Rosetta Stone by Jean-François Champollion
in 1822, the work of translating millions of hieroglyphs from the
plethora of Egypt's historical sites really began.

Successful interpretation of tombs, temples and papyri gained
major impetus after the detailed work of Alan Gardiner (an
English Egyptologist born in 1879) was published in 1927.
His great work, *Egyptian Grammar – Being an Introduction
to the Study of Hieroglyphs*, is the standard textbook of the

language, its last edition being published in 1957. Taken from this book came Gardiner's Sign List, a distillation of the key symbols organized by topics that divide Egyptian life into its key components. The sign list marks each symbol with a unique reference and remains the most commonly used reference.

Hieroglyphs on the walls of one chamber of the Temple of Horus in Edfu.

Reading the Symbols

Here we are attempting to tackle the baffling nature of reading
Egyptian hieroglyphs. Wherever they are found, from Egypt itself
to the great museums of the world, hieroglyphs are seen on
all manner of materials. They always excite and intrigue.
They may be carved on stone and sculptures, painted on wood
and tomb walls, written on papyrus and moulded into precious
metals. The word 'hieroglyph' comes from the ancient Greek
term meaning 'sacred writing'. This short introduction to reading
them suggests ways to understand the complex nature of what
confronts you in an Egyptian tomb or temple, for instance.

There are three key types of hieroglyphs. Firstly, the 'ideogram'
(or logogram). Ideograms represent real things, which would
have been familiar to all Egyptians: an ibex, jackal, hoopoe, the
sun rising over a mountain, a fishing boat and lotus flowers,
perhaps. Hieroglyphs were drawn by trained scribes, often within
a family, and many ideograms were commonly used across the
country. Such wide, and regular, use helped with decoding this
language many centuries later, and these symbols are perhaps
the most accessible way to start reading the language.

*Two hieroglyphs, a bee (symbol for Lower Egypt) and a rush/plant (symbol for Upper Egypt)
here combined with two loaves to represent The King of Upper and Lower Egypt.*

This ideogram hieroglyph represents a clump of papyrus plants quite clearly. It also refers to areas of Egypt linked to water and plant growth, particularly the Egyptian Delta.

An ideogram represented a word in itself, making it easier to remember as well as being familiar in life as a spoken word. Next come the more common symbols that operate as 'phonograms'. These hieroglyphs were critical because each represented a sound or syllable which, when combined, formed a word. For instance, to explain using English, combine the symbol for 'bee' with the symbol for 'leaf'. Together they make a new word, bee-leaf, or belief. We end up with a new spoken word that bears no connection to its components, illustrating how this ancient language evolved to become ever more extensive in vocabulary. The number of possible variations of hieroglyphs was enormous, but the sounds when spoken could often sound similar, making it important to avoid confusion when the hieroglyphs themselves were laid out to read.

As the language evolved the need for extra grammar became important in the form of 'determinatives' to help explain the story or sentence in progress. A determinative is a form of hieroglyph that has no sound itself, but changes or clarifies the meaning of the group of symbols it is attached to. Hieroglyphs commonly used in this way would include 'man' or 'woman', when attached to an event, for instance; it was usual to use an image of a sail to

represent 'air or wind'; or a 'man rejoicing' figure would add a
happy feeling to the event being described. Symbols for 'night'
and 'day' would be critical for storytelling and recording events.
Knowledge of these sign types and the brilliance of those who
recorded Egyptian life and times thousands of years ago give the
visitor to Egypt a small introduction when surveying what they
find in tombs and temples. The cartouche is another word form, a
group of symbols together in an oval loop that contains the name
of a ruler of Egypt, important figures who were rarely shy of
proclaiming their success. Identifying pharaoh's name inside
a cartouche is an accessible starting point for first
reading hieroglyphs.

The task of understanding hieroglyphs 'in situ' is a frustrating
one, as one tries to unravel a collage of ideograms, phonograms
and determinatives. They do operate under rather complex
grammatical principles, and there are exceptions to all rules. It
is important to note that hieroglyphic writing was a functional
language in ancient Egyptian and grew from the need to record
and organize a complex and successfully expanding civilization.

*The tomb of Nefer is within the Pyramid complex of Unas at Saqqara. Nefer held the position
of Director of Singers'. This scene shows him sitting, after death, at his offering table.*

Hieroglyphs were a live language that was controlled by the priesthood, a language whose common use ended, and spoken version was lost, after millennia of development. With the finding of the Rosetta Stone centuries later, vital clues were revealed and decipherment began. What we now understand of this complex society proves that ancient Egypt had an extensive administration and a powerful priesthood, and used hieroglyphs to record the country's history and religion. Everything from the chronology of pharaonic rule and military triumphs, tales of everyday life, to their preoccupation with preparation for a journey to the afterlife. Their stories in pictures are ours to read 5000 years later.

A cartouche inlay that includes the throne name of Seti II as the upper line:
'The Strong One of the Manifestations of Ra, beloved of Amun' (1200–1194 BC).

Life and Land

Although most ancient Egyptians could not read the hieroglyphs that they saw when visiting temples and tombs, this did not mean that only the elite scribal class could take meaning from the language.

Many of the most interesting signs reveal the lives of working Egyptians, their families and the world around them.

A man washing himself, a woman sitting with her child and an eye flowing with tears – all are represented as hieroglyphs.

They could also pick out animals and birds that would have been everyday sights in ancient Egypt, including the hoopoe, which remains common to this day. Staple foods, including emmer wheat, which was used to produce both food and drink, and Bolti fish, would also have been recognizable. The following pages look at more hieroglyphs representing Egyptian life in greater detail.

The River Nile, Egypt's lifeblood for thousands of years.

Sistrum

Symbol:

Represented in hieroglyphic form as a musical instrument
with a handle, the sistrum was a type of rattle that emitted
a tinkling sound, which may have led to its name. It was used
by women in certain rites, often accompanied by the menat.
This rattle was associated with religious ceremonies honouring
the goddess Hathor.

Meaning:

The hieroglyph and the instrument were widely used from the
Old Kingdom onwards, having associations with the mastaba
tombs of King Teti in the Sixth Dynasty. All but the handle of the
sistrum was made from metal. The handle itself was topped with
decorative images of Hathor, often shown on a box or temple,
above which the rattle ring with metal pieces was attached.
One of the most important temples of Hathor is Dendera, where
columns inspired by the sistrum handle shape can still be seen.

The sistrum was a heavy instrument, made of brass or bronze,
and it could be as much as 70cm long, similar in size and shape
to a tennis racket. Variants of the sistrum continued into later
dynasties and also became common outside Egypt during the
Graeco–Roman period.

Bee

Symbol:

This attractive hieroglyph reflects the affection and respect that Egyptians held for bees, the only source of sweetness in the ancient world. The word 'bit' when spoken represented both bee and honey in the ancient Egyptian language. The bee symbol also represented the king of Lower Egypt when combined with bread symbols. Stories that feature bees can be traced back to 3500 years BC, as can evidence of beekeeping in the Nile Delta, a vast area filled with plants and flowers. In one myth, the sun god Re takes tears, being shed by the sun, and turns them into bees to be scattered across the land.

Meaning:

Honey was first farmed using an early pipe made of clay or mud that housed bees in an early type of hive. Over millennia images of beekeeping started to resemble more modern techniques, and scenes of honey collection appear. Honey was eaten both for food sweetening and medical purposes in Egypt, and was used to treat wounds. It was also the basis for beeswax used in religious ceremonies. Honey was widely farmed. Hives were used all year long by the farmers, who moved them up and down the river Nile on special rafts in order to have a year-round supply. Occasionally mummies were embalmed using honey. Some honey, in jars found in tombs, is even still edible.

Lotus

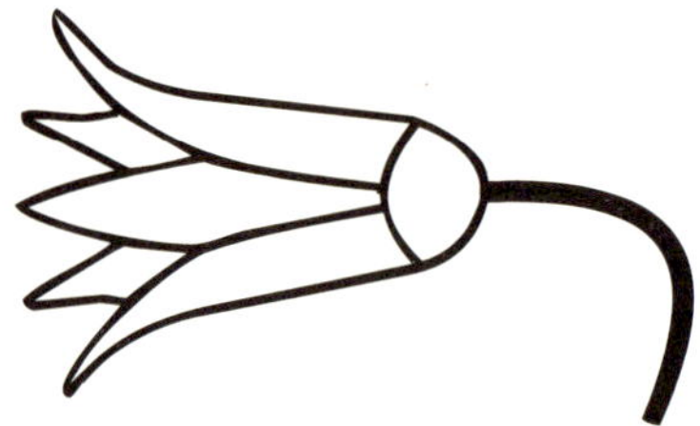

Symbol:

One of the most beloved flowers of ancient Egypt, the shape
of the white or blue Egyptian lotus adorned the past. The lotus
remains popular in present-day Egypt, where its distinctive style
brings instant visual associations with the daily life, history of
art, jewellery and artefacts of thousands of years. The distinctive
smell of the flower was thought to be arousing, emphasizing its
significance to rebirth in life and the afterlife.

Meaning:

The lotus flower hieroglyph represented Upper Egypt, and the
lotus shown in the alphabet is the sacred blue lotus. Once more
we find the cycle of the sun, of day and night, reflected as the
flower closes each dusk and reappears from beneath the water
at dawn. This cycle and the natural beauty of the flower is why it
appears in so many tombs, in scenes of offerings or banqueting,
as a symbol of life and joyous renewal. In the Egyptian Book of
the Dead one spell recommends 'turning oneself into a lotus' for
the time to come in the afterlife.

Today visitors to the tombs and temples of Egypt or the world's
museums find the lotus symbol often framing pictures, walls,
on columns and under the roof of giant spaces. The use of lotus
imagery in gold jewellery is common, creating stunning visual
effects through the use of gemstones within the lotus shape.

The pharaoh Seti I presents sacred lotus flowers to Horus, the falcon-headed god.
Temple of Osiris, Abydos.

Tree of Life

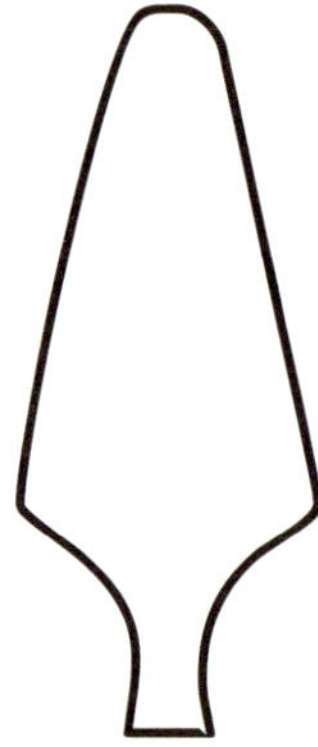

Symbol:

The tree hieroglyph, which depicts a sycamore tree, is a symbol that represents, among other things, destiny and eternal life. It was often connected in groups with other hieroglyphs whose meanings were to do with good fortune and protection. Hieroglyphs using parts of trees, such as branches, represented youth, strength and the time of year.

Meaning:

The idea of the tree of life appears in the mythologies of most ancient civilizations. In Egypt, both in writing and art, trees were portrayed in many forms such as sycamore, acacia or willow.

In one example the tree-goddess Nut can be seen with her legs merging with the sycamore tree. This tree was particularly important for ancient Egyptians because it indicated the presence of water. For this reason the sycamore appears widely in tomb art and was believed to provide fresh food, drink and shade in the afterlife. The tree of life was also believed to grow by the gates of heaven.

Bennu Bird

Symbol:

The Bennu bird was depicted in hieroglyphic form as the outline of a heron (all birds and living creatures were shown in profile except the owl). The heron also features in a hieroglyph standing on a perch, meaning 'innundated'. It was one of several migrating water birds that arrived on the Nile during its annual flooding and are depicted in hieroglyphs, among them ducks and flamingoes.

Meaning:

The Bennu bird was the sacred bird of Heliopolis, where the ben-ben stone of the early creation myth was situated. Its name may have derived from the ancient Egyptian word 'weben', meaning 'to rise' or 'to shine'. The Bennu bird is symbolic of regeneration and resurrection. The Bennu was present at creation, being the first life to appear, its cry marking the very start of time. The cyclic visits of herons to the Nile Valley during the time of flood made them a mystical presence in the eyes of ancient Egyptians. The Bennu became a deity whose role was to represent the soul of the sun god Re, as 'the sun bird'.

Humankind

Symbol:

A single hieroglyph composed of two people is unusual. Here we see the two hieroglyphs for 'man' and 'woman' combined, one behind the other, kneeling and sitting above the vertical lines that indicate a plural use.

Meaning:

Ancient Egyptian society was one of the earliest to be so hierarchical based on status. The upper class included the royal family, landowners and those highest in the administration, the army and the powerful clergy. The middle class were chiefly those who made money trading and creating goods for sale. It is interesting that the hieroglyph for 'humankind', or more broadly 'people', shows a man and woman from the much larger and poorer working classes. A wider interpretation of this hieroglyph is to embrace all lower class working occupations. Few of the unskilled workers who made up this group could read, making this symbol a recognition among the literate that this represented Egypt's majority.

Sema

Symbol:

Sema falls within the category of 'parts of mammals' in the hieroglyphic list and represents a windpipe leading to the lungs. One meaning is indeed 'lung', but it is as a symbol of the word 'unite' that *sema* carries a significant value in Egypt's story. This hieroglyph provides a base to build further symbols upon, which have significant royal and religious meanings.

Meaning:

The simplicity of the *sema* shape is its strong central line (the trachea) from top down. This line, connecting to the lungs, made for a symmetry that could represent union. It's best known as a symbol of the union of Upper and Lower Egypt, with the papyrus and lotus plants placed either side of the symbol, creating a different hieroglyph, known as the *sema-tawy* (meaning Union of the Two Lands). The *sema-tawy* is commonly found on items such as scarabs from the Middle Kingdom onwards. This symbol of unity continued to appear long beyond the existence of a unified kingdom. A further use of *sema* as a central thread shows gods such as Horus and Seth on either side or the land goddesses Wadjet and Nekhbet.

Pregnant Woman

Symbol:

This symbol means both 'pregnant' and 'conceive' . Women are shown in profile with their hair length being the most consistent difference from symbols of men. Other hieroglyphs representing women are few and are mostly confined to their role in bearing and nursing children. In this hieroglyph we see the woman kneeling, rather than sitting, as she awaits the birth of a child. In the most significant hieroglyph of a woman (outside childbearing) a woman with a crown and carrying a plant is used when displaying the name of a queen.

Meaning:

Early medical papyri (circa 2000 BC onwards) show that ancient Egyptians understood the relationship between sex and pregnancy. However, they believed the embryo was created by the man's sperm alone. Contraceptive methods using a wide range of natural remedies to be drunk or eaten were known and tried (such as honey or acacia as spermicides), along with magic spells. Symptoms such as sickness and skin colour were seen as indicators of pregnancy, at which point the gods were called upon for help in determining the eventual outcome.

Infant mortality was high, however, with many families experiencing the loss of children at some time. The gods closely linked to childbirth were Heket and Tawaret. Heket is a frog goddess whose role was to fashion the child in the womb and to oversee the birth as a spiritual midwife. The wider protection of all pregnant women was given by Tawaret, the goddess best known in the form of a hippopotamus.

Statuette of the goddess Tawaret, Ptolemaic period, 332–30 BC.

Horizon

Symbol:

One of the three symbols that show the hills of Egypt is *akhet*. This hieroglyph links land and skies together by showing a sun between the hills as shown in the *djew* symbol (opposite). *Ahket* (literal meaning 'horizon') is a symbol that represents those key moments of each day that were so vital to ancient Egyptians, namely the first and last rays of the sun's daily lifegiving journey. The horizon symbol is linked to the god Hor-em-akhet (another form of Horus), where the *ahket* symbol represented a god of the East, and therefore the rising sun.

Meaning:

This simple, graphic shape was a hieroglyph that was regularly incorporated into amulets and paintings or temple carvings. The *aker* amulet variant of *akhet* is a symbol that blends the shape with two lions whose role is to defend the start and end of the day. Aker was an earth god who carried the barque of the sun on its journey through the night, connecting with sunset and then sunrise. The lions on an amulet look outwards, towards the east and west to greet or bid farewell to the day. Furthermore, the powerful light of the sun over the horizon was seen as a focal point (as it is today across the Nile), leading to the idea of the 'horizon of eternity', where the sun would last forevermore. This expression became associated with tombs in later dynasties, themselves 'houses of eternity'.

Mountain

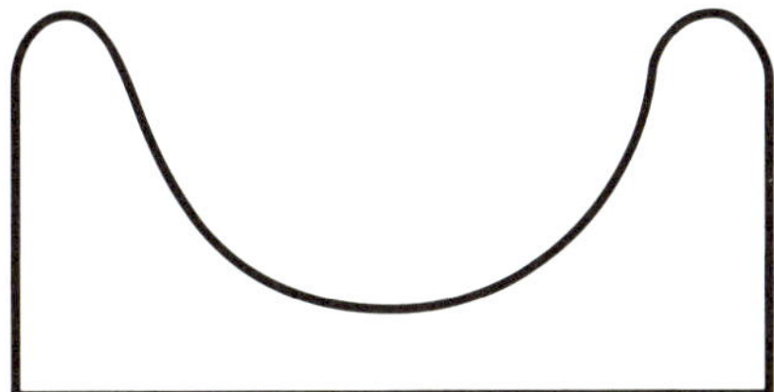

Symbol:

The hieroglyphs for hills or mountains vary, with the outline for mountain (*djew*) showing the two hills and a valley (wadi) in between. The hill shape is applied to all types of upland, relating to anything from a large rocky outcrop to desert peaks and ranges. In hieroglyphic writing this shape is more than a landscape feature, being a representation of the land that bridges the space between earth and above by holding up the sky. Although this sign could represent many hills, it is the Nile valley, shown between the two mountain peaks known to ancient Egyptians as Manu on the west bank and Bakhu on the east.

Meaning:

The concept of distant mountains to Egyptians strongly linked them to the idea of the mortal world's end. People were buried and the afterlife began in the tombs of the west bank, and the hills themselves were protected by lion deities who protected the sun each day.

The *djew* took on wider meanings over time, and was included with symbols to designate the names of other countries or places; in these cases the hieroglyph may have three rather than two peaks. The lands represented by a three-hill hieroglyph were largely seen as 'outside the valley' in dangerous lands associated with evil forces or rough terrain where life was hard to sustain and wild, dangerous animals and creatures lived.

The West

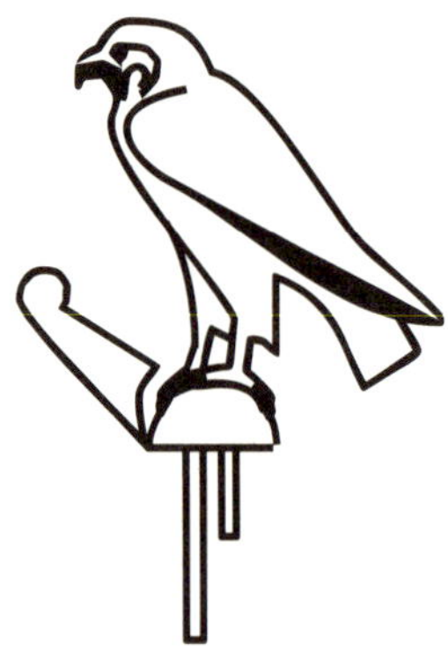

Symbol:

This is the 'Emblem of the West' – a feather, perhaps from an ostrich, atop a pole – and represents the west. The west was important and revered as the region where the dead were buried and then reborn before eternal afterlife. It is referred to as 'the beautiful west' in Egyptian texts. Imentet is goddess of the west and was depicted wearing this hieroglyph as her headdress, linking her to the deceased of the western necropolis in Upper Egypt. Another version of the hieroglyph includes a falcon beside the feather standing on a military standard.

Meaning:

The west illustrated by this symbol takes in the lands beyond Egypt. It appears in representations of western peoples such as the Libyans, shown with this hieroglyph on their heads to illustrate their origins. The adoption of the symbol by the goddess Imentet came with the New Kingdom as she came to be the personification of the many burial centres of Thebes. As goddess of the deceased she was assigned to welcome those who had died with gifts of food and drinks, to give them strength enough for their journey to paradise. Imentet is mentioned frequently in the Books of the Dead and is a deity closely interwoven with major gods and goddesses of the dead such as Hathor and Isis.

The goddess Imentet, adorned by the Emblem of the West, on the wall of the Tomb of Menna on Luxor's west bank.

Headrest

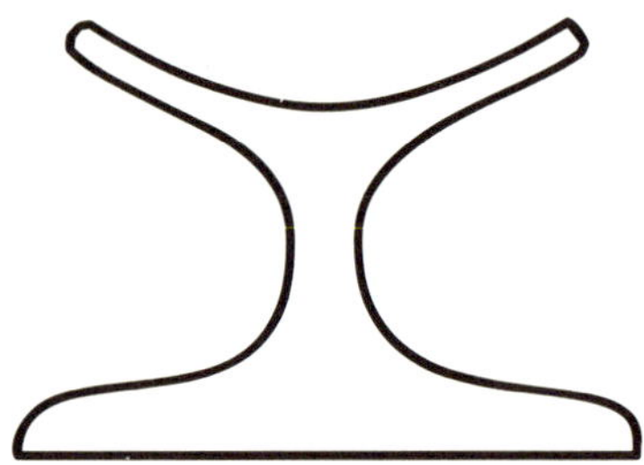

Symbol:

The headrest hieroglyph is a simple shape, reflecting the everyday headrest in many homes. The words 'headrest' and 'pillow' were interchangeable. With a wide and solid base (usually oval or rectangular in shape) and gently curved piece of wood for the face cushion, this symbol appeared over 5000 years ago. Periods of sleep and rest were an important part of daily life in a hot country like Egypt, so the symbol of a headrest, and actual headrests, being found in tombs for millennia is no surprise. In Egypt (and other African countries) this headrest was also for rest in the afterlife, ensuring eternal sleep in the afterlife or providing a platform for resurrection.

Meaning:

Some form of headrest has been in use in Egypt from pre-dynastic times, with examples of simple block forms of elevation being found, and the shape recognized in the hieroglyph has been found in neolithic era archaeology. Headrests were made of many materials, depending on status and wealth. Basic wooden headrests were most commonplace, with ivory a well-used material along with stone. Jewelled semi-precious stones on clay or alabaster were for funerary use, as was beautiful faience. Headrest images appear in many texts and temple art and headrests were themselves inscribed with words and images such as protective spells.

Egg

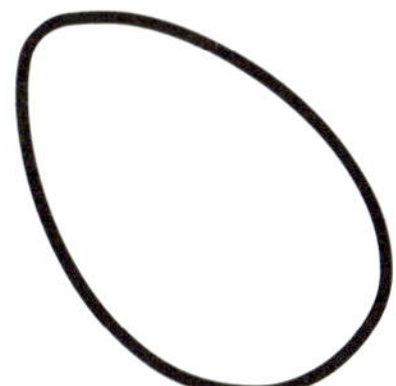

Symbol:

The egg in hieroglyphs is depicted at an angle, ensuring its recognition as more than a symmetrical oval shape without life. As well as representing the eggs of many birds known to ancient Egyptians, the egg was also linked to several goddesses. Their names included eggs in their hieroglyphic identifying block of letters as references to future childbirth. Most notable of these was Isis; this symbol also appears in the royal cartouche of Queen Cleopatra III.

Meaning:

In ancient Egypt the visual tradition assumed round objects or spheres, having no end, were eternal. Similarly eggs, producing chicks, represented resurrection. The egg was part of the ancient Egyptians' diet, most coming from the birds that lived along the Nile. Over time the domestic chicken also became common. However, the egg was rarely shown as food in drawings of Egyptian life.

Sacred birds, especially the ibis, were mummified in their millions in huge burial areas and eggs were placed, wrapped in bandages, alongside them. When multiple coffins were used in burials the innermost one was called the egg. This was believed to be the place from which the dead would be born again.

Sail

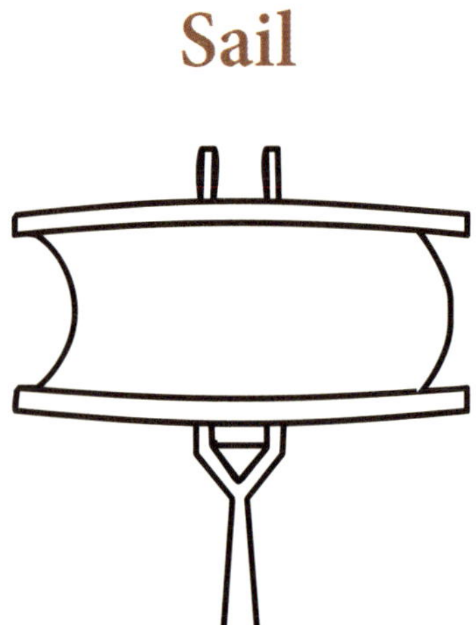

Symbol:

This hieroglyph is a timeless shape that would still resonate with the modern sailor. Ships were a vital part of Egyptian life and society, serving travel, trade and fighting purposes.

This symbol, beyond representing a ship's sail, is associated with other themes. The wind, storms and weather were all important to storytelling, ensuring the sail appears regularly in writings. This sail shape actually represents the Egyptian boats that were used for longer journeys, rather than the traditional felucca sails seen on the Nile today. Given the Nile's flow north and the vagaries of the wind, such boats could be powered by either wind or oars at different times.

Meaning:

Despite Egypt's very settled climate, storm clouds played their part when trips were undertaken, especially the many to other countries for trade. As such, representations of breath, wind, freeze, to be cold and storm all incorporate this hieroglyph. Representations of the role of captain or skipper also include the ship's sail.

The idea of the sailboats carrying the deceased on their journey was a natural extension of the use of boats in mythology. In the Book of the Dead the sail is held in the hand of the deceased,

providing a breath when standing before various gods including
Shu, god of the air. Paintings and papyrus show the use of the
cosmic boat that transports the dead to travel through the night
skies to the world beyond.

Sailing boat, Temple of Horus, Edfu. The hieroglyph closely resembled actual ships,
which changed little over millennia.

Sky

Symbol:

There are many signs depicting elements of the sky and the heavens, such as the sun and moon and stars. This hieroglyph is the literal building block of this group of symbols, representing both the sky and heaven, as well as meaning 'above'. This simple bridge-like shape represents a ceiling supported by corner posts, which is how ancient Egyptians saw the skies.

Meaning:

This representation is drawn from its architectural comparison to buildings, particularly temples, where such a shape was common and the roof represented the sky, heaven or the cosmos in miniature. Variants of the sky hieroglyph include a weather-linked symbol representing rain storm, clouds, dew and rain. There are other signs that mean night or darkness and are connected to the important deity Nut, goddess of the sky, who is also depicted as a woman arched across the heavens, like the sky hieroglyph. Nut was responsible for the sun during the hours of darkness – she swallowed the solar disk at sunset and gave birth to it at dawn, heralding a new day.

Senet Board Game

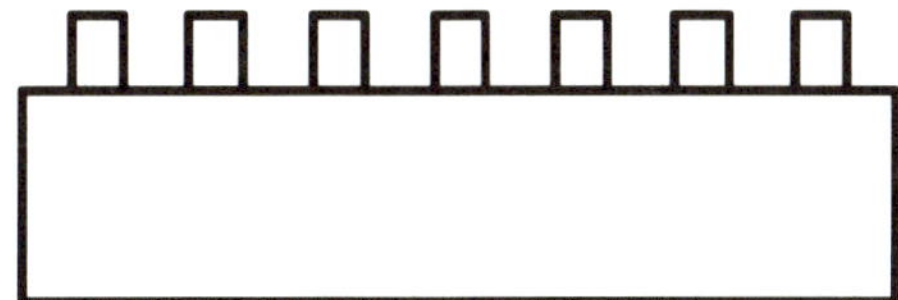

Symbol:

This representation of an ancient Egyptian board game provides a glimpse of daily life. This game is known to have existed through fragmentary evidence from 3100 BC and appears on tomb walls some 500 years later. The shape of the hieroglyph does not reveal the three-dimensional structure of a board, which is more akin to a box of dominoes. When connected to other symbols the senet board usually indicates a sense of established order and strength.

Meaning:

This game became established over many centuries and during the New Kingdom its aim was to show the journey of the *ka* spirit of life into the afterlife, a journey for which all Egyptians were preparing. The game when in play has the appearance of three-dimensional chess, though the rules themselves are not fully known. It is played today based on notes gleaned from different papyri and tomb paintings and retains the elements of luck, strategy and gamesmanship that are the hallmarks of successful board games. Senet was a successful method of widening Egypt's relations with neighbours and it has been identified in use across the Near East, with Cyprus a centre for Senet competition.

Pot

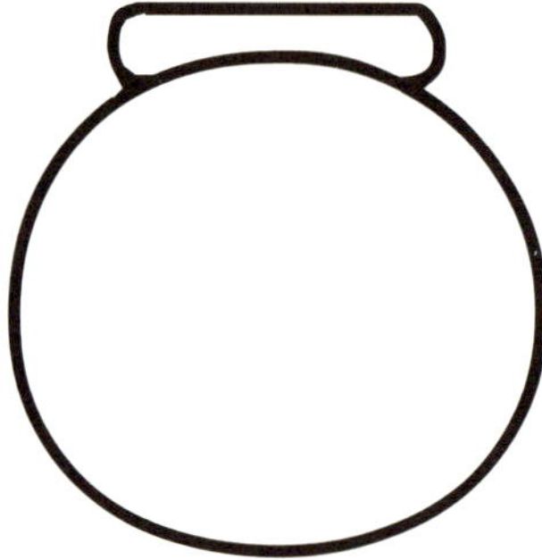

Symbol:

This clay pot is a simple but ubiquitous object in ancient Egypt, and is used in many hieroglyphs. Pots that link to protection, reward and counting are linked to the goddess Nut. She is the embodiment of the vault of heaven and is depicted in paintings with a water-pot on her head. Egypt, a land with natural resources, fostered the development of a rich tradition in ceramics. They yield an unrivalled source for research into Egyptian language, culture and history. Pottery hieroglyphs are found on pre-dynastic ceramics, reflecting the arrival of pottery-making in Egypt, where fine clay vessels were made as early as 5500 BC.

Meaning:

Egyptian pottery was made using clay from two key sources, which determined the base colour of the finished article. Clay that was carried by river from Ethiopia during periods of flood was known as Nile clay, whereas so-called Marl clay came from deposits around oases and the Nile Delta. Marl clay was lighter in colour. Pots were shaped by hand until the earliest potters' wheels, which were driven by hand, arrived sometime in the Fourth Dynasty, coinciding with the pyramid-building era. The art of designing, moulding, painting and glazing ceramic objects was one of ancient Egypt's great artistic legacies.

Leg with Knife

Symbol:

There are more than 10 hieroglyphs that feature legs, and several of these reflect movement, work and daily home life. This example brings the leg together with a knife in a symbol that stands for mutilation, execution, cheating and damage. When grouped with other hieroglyphs it can indicate a place of execution. Knives were used in Egypt from the earliest flint example to the arrival of metal in the First Dynasty. As an object used for protection and defence, their depiction in hieroglyphs is largely associated with killing, revenge and butchery.

Meaning:

The knife symbol commonly appeared in cosmic mythology. Gods such as Re and Thoth are both depicted carrying a blade, a shape which can be both a knife and a crescent moon, in their hands. The knife as protector or weapon is widely seen among representations of gods of the underworld. Deities who defended the sun gods and the solar disk on its journey each night included Bes and Tawaret. Evil creatures can be seen with knife cuts, illustrating their part in the constant battle for supremacy of the underworld. Most frequently knives are shown in the hands of anthropomorphic gods who guard the dead and their shrines.

Religion and Ritual

At the heart of the religion and ritual of ancient Egypt was the belief that society's existence and continuation depended on maintaining a balance or *Maat*. To this end, everyone from the pharaoh to the poorest peasant were expected to take part in festivals and make regular offerings at the temples. The priesthood, which led this system, were a closed community, drawing each new generation from among their own: the control over writing through the scribes was one way this was maintained. Despite the separation, both trainee and mature priests worked in business and administration, and were involved in funerary work, from mummification to burial, all of which activities involved some skill in reading and writing.

Here we see some symbols linked to religious life and work, such as the papyrus scroll and incense bowl, a hieroglyph used to represent a temple or meeting hall, the front of a shrine (where statues of gods were revered) and lastly the half-moon symbol, which was linked to a ceremony held each lunar month.

The walls of the temple of Isis, Philae Island, are splendidly decorated with hieroglyphs and cartouches.

Shen Ring

Symbol:

This hieroglyph, in effect a round form of cartouche, means both eternity and protection. The *shen* ring is represented by a circle of rope crossing itself to create a ring that encircles and protects. The symbol appeared around the Fourth Dynasty and was a popular and steadfast symbol of eternal protection for thousands of years. In the Middle Kingdom this shape begins to be seen in jewellery and amulets for self-protection.

Meaning:

This hieroglyph was closely associated with the god Heh, the god of infinity (and also the word that denoted the number one million). The universal need for protection at all levels of society meant the symbol's use was widespread and it can be found in the tombs of pharaohs and commoners alike. The simple shape was incorporated into all forms of decoration, jewellery or funerary offerings and could be used as a central motif in much more ornate objects. Beside its protective powers the roundness of the shen ring reflects the disk of the sun and its association with the sun god Ra. In tombs and temples it is often seen being carried by gods associated with birds, such as Horus, Mut and Nekhbet.

Menat

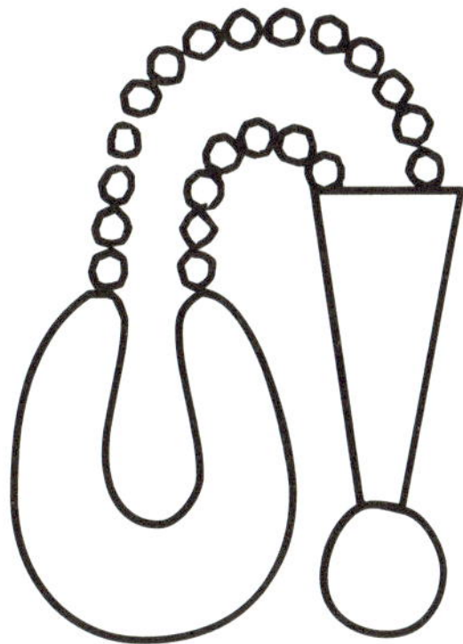

Symbol:

This hieroglyph shows a heavy necklace attached to a
counterpoise, by which it was held during ceremonies and
processions. The necklace would be decorated, often with scenes
relating to birth and featuring Hathor with the infant Horus.
The beaded strings could be rattled in the hand or simply worn.
They were made from various materials such as faience, glass,
lapis lazuli, turquoise and carnelian.

Meaning:

This jewellery was owned or used only by the elite of ancient
Egyptian society or by priestesses at ceremonies linked to the
goddess Hathor. The menat was an important symbol of fertility,
life, rebirth and all aspects of renewal in life and the afterlife.
Such necklaces were in use in the Old Kingdom but became
more familiar in the middle dynasties; they can often be seen in
paintings and hieroglyphs where dancing is taking place. They
were also used as ceremonial offerings to goddesses and may
have been rattled to create music to placate angry gods.
In later times they became more widely used and associated
with a variety of pharaohs and deities. A very fine example
of a menat can be seen in the collection of the Metropolitan
Museum in New York. Known as the Malqata Menat, it was
discovered in 1910.

Djed Column

Symbol:

A popular image meaning strength and stability, the *djed* hieroglyph is a symbol that played a major role in Egyptian life and religion. *Djed* was a sign closely associated with Osiris, and along with the Isis knot (*tyet*), which represented welfare, these hieroglyphs were together seen to stand for the duality of life. As commonly worn amulets of blue and green faience they have a long history, being found in Old Kingdom tombs and associated with the god of creation at Memphis, Ptah. They were often strung across the bodies of mummies because the *djed* was also believed to have regenerative powers.

Meaning:

The symbolism of the *djed* pillar and its importance in myth and life increased through the dynasties. The notion of stability was a vital element of all life in ancient Egypt and it was the role of gods and pharaohs to ensure continuity and safety. The exact nature of the *djed* pillar as shown in hieroglyphs is unclear, though most assume the stem is a tree or vegetation strapped together to create a column; another interpretation is that it may be based on the human backbone. The *djed* pillar played a major role in the anointing of a new pharaoh – a key moment in the rule of a new leader. At the moment the gods passed their powers to the new pharaoh, temple ceremonies took place at which the *djed* pillar was raised from a lain-down position.

It was only at the moment the *djed* pillar was fully upright that order was restored through the arrival of the new king. The wish for continuity ensured amulets were carried by ancient Egyptians, and often buried with them as a potent symbol of safety in the afterlife. A very beautiful *djed* pillar appears in the centre of a gold pectoral found in the tomb of Tutankhamun, lying between the goddesses Isis and Nephthys.

The goddess Isis and pharaoh Seti I shown raising the djed *column, from the walls of Abydos Temple, Upper Egypt.*

Winged Solar Disk

Symbol:

The centrepiece of this symbol is the hieroglyph of the sun disk and two standing cobras, with the spread wings of a bird of prey on either side. This powerful image is commonly seen, large-scale, above doorways or on the ceilings of temples or ceremonial spaces. It is dramatic and intended to project a statement of safety, power and protection.

Meaning:

The idea of the winged sun was a powerful one. Similar iconography can be found in remains across Mesopotamia and Persia, as well as in Anatolia. In Egypt the sun association of this image meant it was linked to the sun god Ra but its origins lie in its association with the god of the midday sun, known as Behdety, who was worshipped in Lower Egypt. Behdety became known as an aspect of Horus over time. In a battle between Horus and the god Seth for control of Egypt it was in the form of a winged sun that Horus protected the kingdom. At the temple of Edfu, Egypt's best-preserved ruin, can be seen a representation of the icon over the entrance.

Scribe's Palette

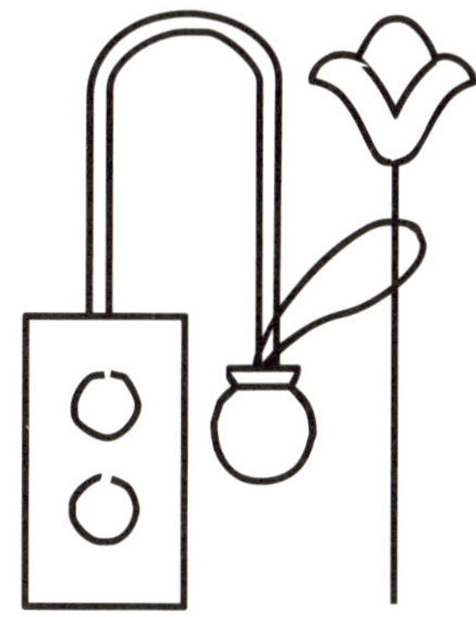

Symbol:

This more complex symbol illustrates tools used by a scribe in ancient Egypt, a position of great honour in their society. Whereas many administrators were able to write and keep records, the role of scribe was elevated and special. The scribe's tools consisted of a wooden or stone palette, usually with a pen slot, two paint depressions and accompanying pigments. They also used a water jug and brush holder for other pens.

Meaning:

Despite the rich legacy of ancient Egyptian papyrus, it is difficult to estimate how many people could read and write in ancient Egypt. The ability to write clearly grew more common over time, with extensive writings, letters and recording of life and business giving historians much to explore, especially from the New Kingdom period. While the literacy levels grew, the role of scribe remained elitist. Scribes guarded their skills and knowledge and ensured they were only shared within palace and temple society, and their family. Schools existed for specialist scribes, in law, administration and medical writing. Importantly, kings, priests and noblemen wrote and had themselves portrayed in the writing position, with book open, to display their skill.

Shrines

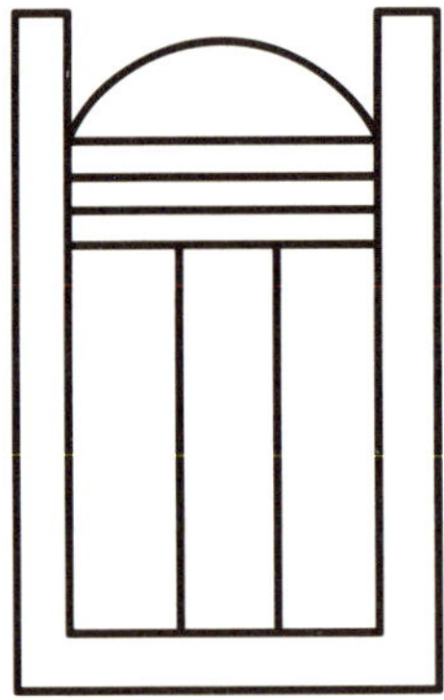

Symbol:

These hieroglyphs represent the national sanctuary buildings of Upper and Lower Egypt. References to these sacred sites appear regularly in archaic documents under the names *pr-nw* and *pr-wr*, and later as hieroglyphs. It is unclear whether these shapes are based on actual buildings, given their complex architecture, though smaller brick structures were in use before the Old Kingdom. These sanctuaries represented the religious cult centre of the vulture goddess Nekhbet in Upper Egypt and the cobra goddess Wadjet in Lower Egypt.

Meaning:

Depictions of shrines in symbol form are rare examples of identifiable buildings in hieroglyphs, emphasizing the importance of such places in daily religious observance and ritual. They served to link people with the gods and the pharaohs. Shrines would contain a statue of the god revered in that temple, usually placed in an inner sanctum, which the priests alone could access. Gifts and prayers were made by visitors to the shrine. In the Book of the Dead a row of such sanctuaries appears, revealing the gods within. Such scenes are replicated in tomb paintings and on papyri.

Upper Egyptian shrines were places of sanctuary associated with Nekhbet, the vulture goddess, shown here at the Temple of Hatshepsut.

Pharaohs and Power

The authority of the ruler in ancient Egyptian society was unquestionable. For some rulers, leaving behind their own mark, and assuring their immortality, could appear almost obsessional.

Among these samples we find the snake symbol of Uraeus, a consistent figure on the crowns of Pharaohs, the crook and flail that represented the pharaohs power over life and the land whilst alive, and crowns of Egypt whose image was central to signifying the rulers power over the country.

The following pages describe in more detail some of the hieroglyphs that were incorporated into regal presentation on state occasions, and those which represented the crowns of Egypt, vital symbols for ensuring recognition of a ruler's position while they were alive.

Pyramids at Giza.

Uraeus

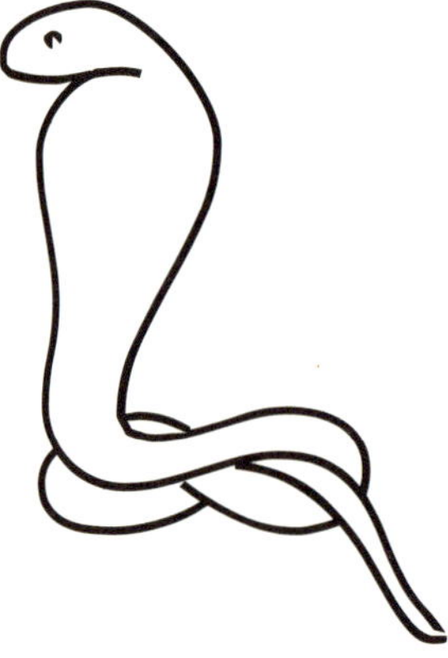

Symbol:

The hooded cobra is a powerful and fiery symbol of gods and pharaohs throughout ancient Egypt's chronology; most notably, associated with the goddess Wedjat. It was also used in the headdress of the sun god Re. Due to her links with the Delta city of Buto, the cobra in striking mode also represented Lower Egypt. The snake was a symbol of protection in both life and the afterlife, based on the fact of their spending time in cool dark places and attacking dangerously when provoked.

Meaning:

The uraeus (a Greek word which may have its origins in the early Egyptian expression 'she that rears up') holds a position of significance among ancient Egypt's symbols. Its connection with the Wedjat eye is evidence of the snake's protection of the ruler, signifying the pharaoh was her chosen one, and as a powerful mark of both royalty and authority. A familiar part of pharaonic representation, it was perhaps most famously seen on the headdresses of Rameses the Great and Tuthmose III, two of Egypt's greatest rulers. The uraeus was generally seen by the kings and queens of Egypt as portraying their power over life and death. As a motif, the cobra appears on artefacts of all kinds. In addition the cobra is represented spitting fire to protect the gates of the underworld.

Hooded cobra reliefs adorn Kom Ombo temple, by the Nile between Aswan and Luxor.

Crook and Flail

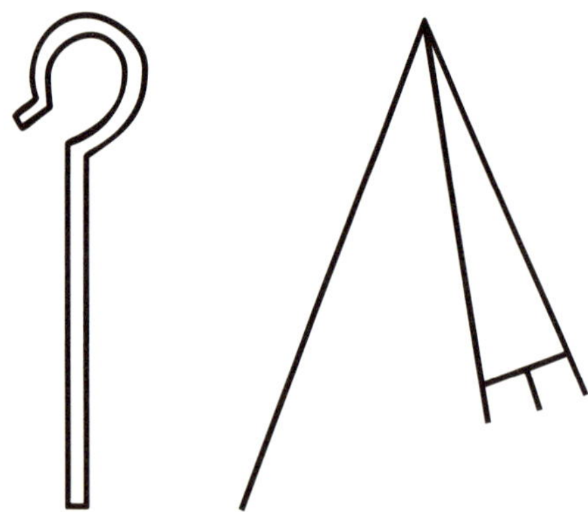

Symbol:

These two objects were important representations of the power of ancient Egypt's rulers but are often shown in the hands of gods as well. These items have their origins in agriculture and are a reminder that the pharaohs' power was derived from the natural wealth of the land. The crook (called the *heka* in Egyptian) developed from the staff held by shepherds into a tool for controlling animals. The flail (*nekhakha*) was a whip used to protect sheep or as a means of keeping away insects but also, in the hands of gods, became a way to ward off evil.

Meaning:

The crook and the flail were commonly used symbols which over time began to be seen together and acquired the position of royal ornament and power. In the hands of both pharaohs and gods, they became seen as an inseparable duo. The crook and flail symbols are common in cartouches and represent royal jurisdiction. Pharaohs carried the two at public events, crossed over the chest, a sight familiar for many dynasties of Egyptian art. The crook and flail were carried or by the pharaoh's side till death and were buried alongside them. In the realm of gods, they were usually seen in the hands of Osiris, the god of the dead and a former king of Egypt.

Pharaohs were often shown carrying the crook and flail, emphasizing their power and strength, as here at the temple of Horus at Edfu.

Hedjet Crown

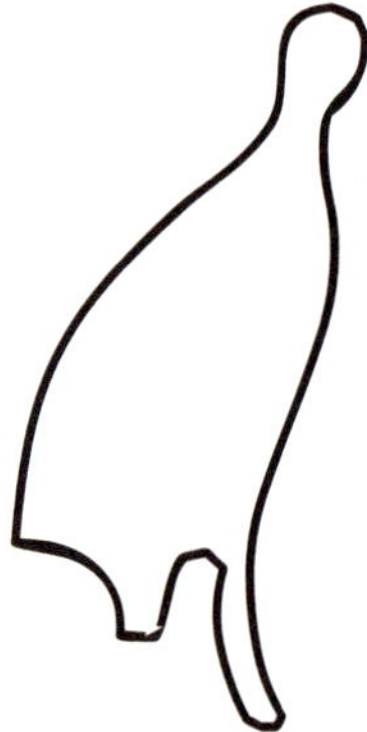

Symbol:
This hieroglyph is a representation of the white crown worn by the kings of Upper Egypt as early as pre-dynastic times. Such rulers (and gods such as Osiris and Nekhbet) were depicted throughout Middle and southern Egypt from Memphis to what is now called Aswan. The red crown (known as *deshret*) was its Lower Egypt equivalent.

Meaning:
Although no physical evidence of the crown exists, the image of the *hedjet* or white crown is commonplace and widespread. It is shown on artefacts dating from around 3200 BC in Nubia, close to the Sudanese border. Perhaps most famously, the crown features on the Narmer Palette. This important discovery from Hierakonpolis depicts King Narmer vanquishing foreign enemies with a mace. The pose is known as 'the icon of majesty' and became a standard representation of royal victory for dynasties to come, appearing on walls and temples until the Roman era. The Narmer Palette is significant because it shows some of the earliest hieroglyphic inscriptions known and is one of the first objects to show ancient Egypt as unified under one ruler.

Pschent Crown

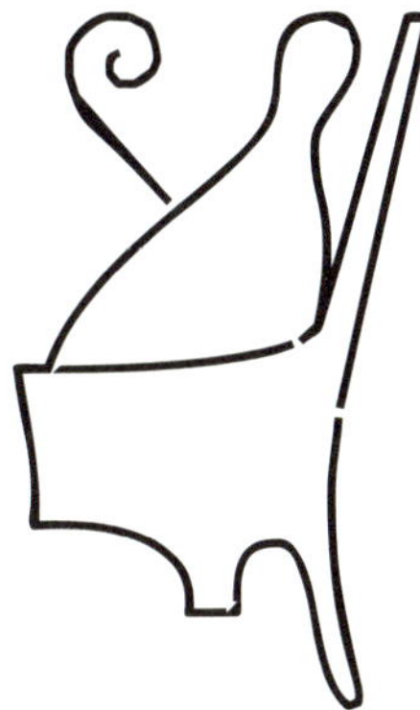

Symbol:

This representation of the joint crowns in one headdress of Upper and Lower Egypt shows the unification of Egypt under one ruler. The *pschent* was more usually referred to as *sekhemty* or 'the two powerful ones'. The double headdress was worn by Egypt's rulers from the time of King Narmer.

Meaning:

In addition to the standard hieroglyph as shown, it was common in paintings and sculpture to find the cobra (uraeus) and the Egyptian vulture (Nekhbet) attached to this crown. This suggested a more powerful ruler.

Gods were shown wearing the double crown, symbolizing their divine right to rule Egypt through the pharaoh – for example, Horus, a major deity with multiple powers, was shown wearing the *pschent* as god of kingship. Representations of Horus are widespread and monumental, with depictions as falcon (or falcon-headed) commonplace. A collosal granite statue of Horus dating from the Ptolemaic period and wearing the *pschent* can be seen in the temple of Edfu in Egypt.

Obelisk

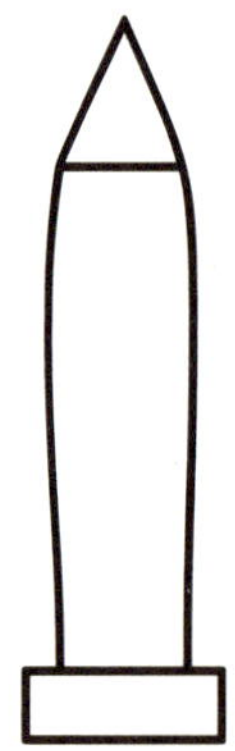

Symbol:

The unmistakable shape of the obelisk ensures this hieroglyph is straightforward to interpret. The word meaning 'obelisk' originated from the Greek word *obeliskos*, which is used in Herodotus's description of his travels in Egypt. In ancient Egypt the word used was *tekhen*, a term which itself had other meanings. This unique shape from ancient Egypt has inspired many recent monuments and remains a favourite and fascinating historical object.

Meaning:

The obelisk has a long history, which began as early as the Fifth Dynasty, and the first monolithic stone was worshipped in Heliopolis, where sun temples were devoted to Ra. These were short pyramid-like objects known as ben-ben stones and shaped as the tip of later obelisks. Their purpose is the subject of many interpretations, all connecting them to the rays of the sun. In later times, when the obelisk had become a much taller monument, they were built under specific orders of pharaohs only, in their capacity as manifestation of the sun gods on earth. It was not unusual for temples in the New Kingdom to have two obelisks to represent the sun–moon cycle of each day. In the case of the temple of Amun at Karnak, four were built. There was a direct relationship between obelisks and the sexual potency in ancient Egyptian religion, where fertility was a key theme in all life.

Queen Hatshepsut's obelisk in Karnak Temple, Luxor, is the second tallest existing in the world and is covered in hieroglyphs.

Was Sceptre

Symbol:

The *was* sceptre is a simple image of a staff topped by an animal's head and with a forked lower end which represents a creature's feet; in life and religion the *was* sceptre was carried by gods and pharaohs alike. Its use indicated that its holder, whether a ruler or the gods, held power over their worlds. Closely associated with Upper Egypt, the *was* sceptre was used to represent the nome (territorial division) for Thebes when pictured with a piece of cloth or a feather.

Meaning:

As a symbol of royal strength the *was* sceptre represented many powers. It protected the deceased in their tombs and represented authority. It was also a symbol of the king's or gods' ability to bring wealth and happiness. In the hands of gods it was a powerful and magical tool. The *was* sceptre was made of wood and decorated with faience, and could also include gold or precious metals. It was also an amulet for protection and in myth four *was* sceptres could be used to support the sky. Many gods were portrayed holding the sceptre incuding Sati, an Upper Egyptian goddess who protected Egypt's southern border, and Sopdu, a bird god who defended the east. The *was* sceptre is also a familiar sight depicted in the hands of gods such as Isis, Hathor and Ptah.

The falcon-headed god Horus carrying the was *sceptre and wearing the white crown of Upper Egypt (Kom Ombo temple).*

Bull

Symbol:

The bull in general was one of several hieroglyphic representations of cattle, animals that were of practical and symbolic importance in ancient Egypt. This bull in fighting stance was a symbol of strength and also represented the idea of kingship. In ancient times, cattle roamed wild and were dangerous and feared creatures. Thus the fighting bull represented the frightening presence of a pharaoh on the battlefield.

Meaning:

Marking the reverence with which ancient Egyptians held cows and bulls, they used the term 'the cattle of god' as an expression for the whole of humankind. The most sacred animal in ancient Egypt was recorded from the earliest texts onwards and was called the Apis bull, though was not shown in its rampant, fighting stance. Only one such named bull was worshipped at any time and it was chosen with great care by priests, based on the bull's markings and shape. This bull was revered through life as the physical manifestation of the god Ptah and after death was buried with previous Apis bulls in underground catacombs, the best-known of which is the Serapeum at Saqqara. In this gigantic tomb each bull was contained in a huge granite sarcophagus.

*Relief of a powerful bull from the Louvre Museum collection, Third Intermediate Period,
which followed the New Kingdom.*

Royal Cartouches

During their lives, pharaohs enjoyed several
names, usually variants on a strong theme.
These names adorned walls and objects and
eventually their tombs, in the form
of a cartouche.

In this section the cartouches of a selection
of Egypt's most famous pharaohs and their
consorts are illustrated, their meanings
explained and their lives explored.
These include Tutankhamun, Nefertari
and Rameses the Great.

All Egyptian rulers were believed to be the
living manifestation of the god Horus, which
was reflected in one of their many names. The
name that was used for the cartouche is known
as the throne name. The standard, empty, royal
cartouche shape is itself also a hieroglyph.

Tutankhamun enjoyed several names. This cartouche presents his birth name:
'The Living Image of Amun, ruler of Southern Heliopolis'.

Khufu

The Great Pyramid of Khufu, the only remaining monument of the seven wonders of the ancient world, is named after the pharaoh Khufu. This is a shortening of his cartouche, which carries the message Khnum-khufei', meaning 'he [Khufu] protects me/us'. Although archaeological evidence of his reign is minimal, Khufu's legacy does include cartouches bearing his name found within the pyramid itself. The best-known representation of Khufu the pharaoh is a 7.5cm (3in) statuette of him sitting on his throne, also bearing his name. Khufu dedicated his time as pharaoh to building one monument in preparation for his journey to the afterlife. The administration, organization and hard work involved in building his pyramid is believed to have been mirrored in the society of his time. As the Old Kingdom's most successful period both for its pharaohs and for developing a sophisticated society, the pyramid era played a vital role.

Khufu built the Great Pyramid using the knowledge passed from his father, Sneferu, who had been able to develop the techniques of pyramid building at Dashur, site of the Red and Bent Pyramids. Khufu is the established Egyptian name for a ruler often referred to as called Cheops (or Suphis) in the writings of the Greek traveller Herodotus. The length of Khufu's reign is disputed, but estimated to be some 24 years. References to his rule reveal only snapshots of the man, but his cartouche and name appear in places as far apart as the Sinai and Aswan, the latter of which was a site used to quarry the red granite used for much building. Along with the pyramid being created for his immortal memory, Khufu also commissioned two boats, known as the Solar Boats, to carry him on his journey to the afterlife. These were discovered under the Giza plateau in 1954, and one of the boats was painstakingly rebuilt and displayed in a specially built hall at Giza.

Bas-relief depicting Princess Meritites, Old Kingdom, Fourth Dynasty, ca. 2500 BC. It shows the two daughters of Meritites and Akhtihetep, flanking a cartouche composed of two cords and bearing the name of the Pharaoh Khufu.

Senusret III

Royal cartouches represent two versions of a king or queen – the throne name and birth name. Here we see the birth name of Senusret III. During their life, a ruler may have several names, but only these two variants would be enclosed in a cartouche. The various name types (known as the royal titulary) are as follows in the case of Senusret III:

Horus name, the oldest known form of a pharaoh's name and the equivalent of a heraldic crest at the time of being made ruler. For Senusret III this is Kheper, or 'The golden Horus has been created'.

Then comes the **Nebty name**, also connected to the new king's appointment and the heraldic goddesses Nekhbet and Wadjet, who represent Upper and Lower Egypt respectively. For Senusret III this name is Netjeri Mesut, meaning 'The Two Ladies, divine of birth'.

The **throne name** is the most significant cartouche, used throughout the pharaoh's time as ruler and appearing most often on walls and statues or amulets, and later in tombs. Shown here is the cartouche for Senusret III. It says Kha-khau-Ra or 'the Kas of Ra have come into being'.

A **birth name** cartouche for Senusret III helps explain how a ruler's name was changed through age and responsibility. The birth name was simply Senusret in hieroglyphs, meaning 'Man of Wosret'.

The Middle Kingdom is seen as a period of stabilization following a time when the pharaoh's power had been threatened by the strength of local rule and the potential division of Egypt into smaller territories. King Senusret III was among those who set Egypt back on the path to unity under one ruler, renewed the role of temples and the priesthood by investment in building, and regained control of Egypt's borders through military power.

Senusret II had been the fourth of the 12th Dynasty kings and
had moved the royal burial grounds away from the area of
Dahshur to El-Lahun in the Fayum, where his pyramid was
built at a new necropolis. This city then served as the political
capital of Egypt until the end of the 13th Dynasty. He seems
to have focused on ruling in harmony with his governers and
improving agriculture. This period of relative stability continued
under Senusret III, who ruled for 37 years and remodelled
Egypt's administration through centralization. The Fayum area
(south-east of modern Cairo) continued to expand as well as
becoming a major necropolis for rulers and high officials.

Senusret III also brought more military success, with campaigns
in Nubia and Syria. The income from plunder was considerable,
and was used to renew the tired temple infrastructure
throughout Egypt. Senusret III also oversaw major engineering
work, including the clearing of a large canal at Aswan, which
opened a channel past the First Cataract, ensuring his ships
had access to Nubia for both trade and military reasons. The
southern defences of Egypt were also settled during the Middle
Kingdom, with the building of fortresses as far as the Second
Nile Cataract, effectively a new border with Nubia.

*A lintel with hieroglyphs. The cartouche of Senusret III can be seen in the middle of the relief
(Karnak, 12th Dynasty, 1878–1841 BC).*

Tuthmose I

Tuthmose I ruled for a relatively short period but his legacy was far reaching. He was not from a royal family, but succeeded Amenhotep I, having possibly served as a co-regent in Amenhotep's later years, and married his daughter Ahmose. He is recognized for his military campaigns outside Egypt and for extending the temple complex of Karnak in Luxor. Tuthmose I is also believed to have been the first pharaoh buried in what became the Valley of the Kings, though his mummy was removed at a later date, and discovered with other rulers of the 18th Dynasty in Deir el-Bahri.

Like many pharaohs he ensured his achievements in life were celebrated in buildings, monuments and art. Statues and obelisks emphasized this position, and the enlarging of Karnak helped strengthen the power of the priesthood during the New Kingdom at Thebes. Tuthmose I ensured his successful army campaigns, which reached as far as the Euphrates in Mesopotamia, were known to all Egyptians through his state-sponsored building programmes. To Egypt's south the conquering of Nubia extended the pharaoh's political and economic power deep into Africa. This included control over rich gold deposits at a time when this precious metal was especially prized. At the same time the Kushites were a persistent and menacing threat to Egypt's southern border and Tuthmose moved decisively to secure his territory as far south as the Third Cataract.

Tuthmose was the father of the future Queen Hatshepsut. Her temple remains one of the largest monuments on the west bank of modern-day Luxor. The royal cartouche came into common use to illustrate the names of Egypt's kings and queens from the late Third Dynasty onwards. They are oval shaped with a line extended at one end, like a rope.

Pharaohs had more than one name, though only two of
those would be found in cartouche form, but not in the same
cartouche. The first cartouche used the 'nomen' – essentially
the first name, given at birth. Later the 'prenomen' came to
represent the living pharaoh; this is usually referred to as the
throne name. Both names could appear on objects side by side,
perhaps on a sarcophagus, a throne or amulets. In the case of
Tuthmose I, his throne name was Akheperkare, meaning 'Great
is the Manifestation of the Soul of Ra', and that title is illustrated
here. The throne name is pronounced as Aa-Kheper-Ka-Ra.

Scarab inscribed with the throne name of Tuthmose I: 'Great is the Manifestation of the Soul of Ra'.

Hatshepsut

Hatshepsut was one of only three female pharaohs in ancient Egypt, and today evidence of her building and art referencing her ensure her position as a royal icon. Her best-known cartouche portrays her as being 'Horus, powerful of Kas, lord of East and West, a pious lady and golden falcon, divine in her rings, King of Upper and Lower Egypt daughter of Re, Hatshepsut, who is joined with Amun'. Hatshepsut had been the wife of powerful pharaoh Thutmose II and borne him a son. Thutmose II died unexpectedly when the child was very young, which led to Hatshepsut ruling as regent for the son.

Despite her successors' efforts to erase her from memory, the evidence of her powerful role ruling Egypt alongside her son, survives. She is also presented in her semi-divine nature as the daughter of the god Amun, the supreme god in the pantheon of deities. This bestowed on Hatshepsut the power of pharaoh. Visitors to the west bank of Thebes today all stand in awe of the giant temple of Hatshepsut, her greatest creation. This unique piece of funerary architecture took 15 years to build in the cliff face at Deir el-Bahri. Hatshepsut called this 'a garden for my father Amun'. The magnificent obelisks built in her name at Karnak Temple were to affirm her rule as pharaoh as legitimate by Amun. In the many religious buildings across Egypt that she commissioned, Hatshepsut was known to perform rituals previously reserved to male pharaohs, thus emphasizing her role as king. In paintings Hatshepsut is shown wearing male clothes over a masculine body.

Hatshepsut statue base, New Kingdom, c. 1479–1458 BC.

Queen Tiye

Despite not ruling Egypt in her own right, Queen Tiye, as the most powerful wife of pharaoh Amenhotep III, played important roles as consort, involving herself in both domestic and foreign policy. Her image and name appear widely on all forms of art, buildings and correspondence from the era. This was despite the large number of wives in competition with her, not all of whom were from Egypt and indeed some of whom were princesses from lands that shared good relations with Egypt at the time. Her cartouche, as queen consort, often appears alongside the king's, as we can see on this jar.

She had many titles including 'Hereditary Princess', 'Sweet of Love', 'Lady of the Two Lands' and 'King's Wife, his beloved'. The queen's more pharaoh-like title 'Mistress of Upper and Lower Egypt' suggests the depth of her involvement in policy and influence on her husband. Amenhotep III enjoyed a successful reign during one of the New Kingdom's most prosperous times, and Egypt was enjoying cordial relationships with its neighbours. The role of queen therefore allowed for patronage of the arts, culture and manufacture. The sheer amount of highest-quality artefacts recovered from this era is enormous. The amount of new temples, monuments and tombs to be decorated meant a flowering of the hieroglyphic art as the highly trained scribes grew in number. This period provides the modern visitor to Egypt with a wealth of ancient writings to explore, with high-quality carving and much more extensive vocabulary of symbols used to tell the pharaoh's own story.

Amenhotep III and Queen Tiye were skilled communicators. It was not uncommon for detailed accounts of their triumphs to be distributed to the people of ancient Egypt in the form of scarabs covered in hieroglyphs to be enjoyed by those who could do so, and read out loud to those who could not. News of both the king and Queen Tiye (again emphasizing her pre-eminent role in his household) was spread this way. On

the occasion of their wedding, for example, news was spread
by scarab to all Egyptians. Tiye was named 'Great Royal Wife'
alongside the names of her parents.

After the death of her husband, Queen Tiye's son
Amenhotep IV took the reins. When Amenhotep IV came to
power, his initial throne name and cartouche were given as
Nefer-Kheperu-Ra, 'The beautiful one of the manifestations
of Ra, the unique one of Ra' . However, Tiye's son was a deep
thinker and philosopher, determined to break the mould of
Egypt's religious establishment. He abandoned all the gods of
the ancient Egyptian religion and declared there to be only one
god, Aten. In time the centre of Egypt's religion was moved
to a new site, called Akhetaten (now known as Amarna), and
the pharaoh called himself Akhenaten. His birth cartouche
was changed, from Amenhotep, god and ruler of Thebes, to
Akhenaten, the Living Spirit of the Aten.

Kohl jar inscribed with the names of Amenhotep III and Queen Tiye.

Tutankhamun

The fame associated with this short-lived pharaoh who ruled for less than 10 years far outweighs his status in life. His arrival, however, helped mark the return to orthodoxy and the end of the monotheistic experiment of the 'heretic king' Akhenaten, believed to be Tutankhamun's father. The boy king's cartouche means 'Living Image of Amun, Ruler of Upper Egyptian Heliopolis', whereas at birth he was named Tutankhaten, 'Living Image of the Aten'. This subtle yet significant change marked the return to polytheism as supported by the religious elite. Tutankhamun is possibly ancient Egypt's most famous figure, at least in popular culture, where his tomb's treasures have come to represent the riches of ancient Egypt in public imagination. Although his story was short – he died before he reached 20 – his reign came during a period of huge change in ancient Egyptian society as his priests re-established the bedrock of Egypt's religious identity.

Despite his early death the treasures found by Howard Carter in his tomb are the largest collection ever found of one pharaoh. Many theories abound regarding his burial and the possibility that Tutankhamun died suddenly is a common belief. This is based on the chaotic nature of the objects strewn around his tomb. These thousands of treasures feature many hieroglyphs and this young pharaoh's life story draws millions of visitors to Egypt.

This gold and faience cartouche from the throne of Tutankhamun bears his birth name:
'the Living Image of Aten'.

Seti I

With the throne name Men-Maat-Ra, or Eternal is the Truth of
Ra, Seti I rule Egypt for just 13 years. Seti I came to the throne
with plans to return Egypt to a more settled and traditional
religious governance. The Amarna pharaohs were still fresh
in the minds of an unsettled population and Seti I was keen
to build new temples devoted to Egypt's wide pantheon of
traditional gods. His cartouches and seals illustrate his message
of stability and strength. Seti I was proclaimed 'the strong bull
who sustains the two lands'. As the father of Rameses II his
influence over the 19th Dynasty was to set in motion a period of
great success on the battlefield and in building a country of such
power and sophistication that it is considered the golden age of
ancient Egypt's story.

Seti I was a remarkable builder and promoter of art. During his
13-year reign some of the New Kingdom's greatest monuments
and art were created. Karnak, perhaps the world's greatest
surviving temple, was begun during his reign and was extended
by others for over 2000 years. His own tomb in the Valley of the
Kings is a masterpiece and the Cenotaph Temple of Seti I
at Abydos features some of the most stunning and colourful
bas-reliefs from the New Kingdom. The temple and hypostyle
retain much of its original grandeur and colour.

The art depicting Seti I with Horus and Osiris is outstanding
and in seven smaller chapels other gods such as Ptah, Amun,
Isis and Ra-Harakhty are venerated. The temple contains one
of the few remaining king lists, showing the cartouches of
Egypt's pharaohs in chronological order. Its hieroglyphs provide
a chronology of ancient Egyptian rule from Narmer, usually
described as the founder of Egypt, until Seti I himself.

Birth and throne cartouches of Seti, from a wall painting of a pillar at the Tomb of Seti I, Valley of the Kings, Western Thebes. (New Kingdom, 19th Dynasty, 1290–1279 BCE.)

Rameses II

Son of pharaoh Seti I, Rameses II became pharaoh at the age of 25 and ruled for 67 years, known now as Rameses the Great. Visitors to Egypt today find themselves surrounded by temples, obelisks and writings that record his years as king. His most famous buildings include the Abu Simbel temples in Nubia, the Ramesseum in Thebes and major work in both Karnak and Luxor Temples. Rameses' name shows devotion to the god Ra, the main god of the sun who is the creator of all the cycles of Egyptian life. The solar disk in his cartouche represents Ra.

Rameses' throne name was User-Maat-Ra, meaning the justice of Ra is powerful. His name is referenced in multiple other hieroglyph variants from his own period and beyond. Rameses II is thought to have had more than eight wives and official records show more than 100 children as his offspring. In the Valley of the Kings a vast tomb (numbered KV5) was discovered containing the sons of Rameses II, a unique find and the largest tomb yet found in Egypt.

Rameses' long reign and supreme power give the opportunity to look more deeply at the many ways a pharaoh may be named during their lifetime. The throne name is generally the one in their royal cartouche. Separate cartouches also contained a royal child's birth name. Other groups of hieroglyphs were simply used to praise pharaohs and Rameses II, given his long reign and fame, was called by many titles. The first form of a royal name in life was termed the Horus name and would compare to what might be called a heraldic crest in more modern history. Here are some examples of Rameses II's Horus names:

– The strong bull, beloved of Ra.
– The strong bull, beloved of Ra, who has trampled foreign countries under his sandals.
– The strong bull, who has governed the Two Lands.
– The strong bull rich in immeasurable years.

Often a pharaoh may be assigned a Nebty name, signifying their power over Egypt, linked to the goddesses Nekhbet and Wadjet. In Rameses II's case his all-encompassing rule ensured many names praising his strength and leadership:

– He who has fought for millions, a stout-hearted lion.
– The divine image of Khepri.
– Who had fought with his strong arm, the protector of his armies.

This cartouche uses a throne name variant of Rameses II: the Justice of Ra is powerful, chosen of Ra. From the temple of Seti I, Luxor.

Nefertari

Nefertari (or Nefertari Meritmut, meaning 'beautiful companion and beloved of Mut') is the name in her cartouche. Mut was the goddess wife of Amun and the great queen of the Theban gods. Nefertari was first in standing among the wives of Rameses II (the Great) and, although little is known of Nefertari's background, her role as chief queen of one of Egypt's greatest rulers was a decisive one. Her significance as queen and her longevity were celebrated in the most beautiful tomb of the Valley of the Queens, which was discovered in 1904 by Ernesto Schiaparelli and restored to its full glory by the Getty Conservation Institute from 1986 to 1992. Its extraordinary painted walls and magnificent chambers stand as testament to her importance. The walls feature many hieroglyphic writings, including chapters from the Book of the Dead.

Although it's believed that Rameses fathered over 100 sons and daughters, it was Nefertari who bore him his first son, and possibly three further boys and two daughters. Among the many monumental temples built in the reign of Rameses the Great, the two temples of Abu Simbel, the smaller of which was dedicated by him to his Queen Nefertari and the goddess Hathor, are perhaps the best known.

Nefertari played a major role in the affairs of state and Egypt's success. A letter written to the Hittite Queen (the Hatti) Padukhepa says: '…and you have written to me about the matter of peace and brotherhood between the great king of Egypt and his brother, the great king of Hatti. May the sun god [of Egypt] and the storm god [of Hatti] bring you joy and may the sun god cause the peace to be good…'

She carried many titles through her life, among them Lady of The Two Lands, Wife of the Strong Bull, God's Wife and Great of Praises; and her husband himself named her 'the one for whom the sun shines'.

Her tomb is testament to one of ancient Egypt's most enduring royal relationships, on a scale to reflect pharaoh's importance. For those wishing to read hieroglyphs it offers great opportunities, thanks to its expert restoration and the limited number of visitors allowed each day.

Tomb wall painting of Queen Nefertari, with her cartouche as the great royal wife of Rameses II.

Alexander the Great (III)

Alexander the Great is one of the greatest figures in history
but less known as an Egyptian pharaoh. He became king of
Macedonia at the age of 20 following the death of his father,
Philip II. Having conquered the Persians at the Battle of Issus,
Alexander turned south to enter Egypt. On arrival he travelled
to visit the oracle of Amun in the Oasis of Siwa, a pilgrimage
which ensured his recognition as a legitimate figure to lead
Egypt as pharaoh. His throne name was then Mery-amun
Setep-en-re (beloved of Amun, chosen by Re).

His military fame as Alexander the Great ensured his arrival
was seen as a divine intervention in the usual pharaonic order
and, while travelling to Siwa, he was welcomed amid great
proclamation and assumed to be a divine saviour. He was made
pharaoh and enjoyed several hieroglyphic names:

– The guardian of Egypt.
– The sturdy-armed one.
– The lion, great of might, who takes possession of mountains,
lands and deserts.

Alexander the Great's time in Egypt was short-lived as pharaoh
but his legacy was long-lived. The wider influence of Alexander's
empire brought Egypt into the Mediterranean sphere of
influence. The founding of Alexandria (Iskandera) marked a
shift in regional power and the city grew to rival Rome.

Cartouche of Alexander the Great (upper right), King of Upper and Lower Egypt (332–333 BC).

Cleopatra VII

There are few names in history that resonate through history as much as Egypt's final pharaoh, Cleopatra. Her cartouche and throne name translates as 'Cleopatra, goddess, beloved of her father'. She held other titles, including 'Mistress of Upper and Lower Egypt' and 'Great of Sceptre'. The Ptolemaic dynasty saw Greek culture and language become dominant and the religion of ancient Egypt was slowly replaced by the beliefs of the Graeco–Roman world.

When Cleopatra became queen, Rome was the ruling power of the region, and she understood the threat to Egypt. Cleopatra set out to ensure Egypt's independence through a complex plan of political alliances. Her relationship with Julius Caesar resulted in the birth of a child, Ptolemy XV Caesarion, and following Caesar's assassination she returned to Egypt. There she became co-regent of Egypt with her half-brother Ptolemy XIV Philopater.

Soon after, Mark Antony met Cleopatra and were married and had children. Mark Antony's feud with the Roman leader Octavian led him to be defeated at the Battle of Alexandria in 30 BC and a year later, believing Cleopatra herself had died, Antony committed suicide. Soon after this Cleopatra, refusing to yield to Roman rule, also committed suicide.

Cleopatra's fame and longevity as a historical figure is partly a product of her untimely death. Tales of her life were published by Roman writers, who magnified them into dramatic tales of sex, power and greed. Having captured popular imagination, these stories were then painted by artists of the Renaissance as well as dramatized by Shakespeare and then in modern film. It is therefore ironic that this enduring symbol of Egypt was herself born a Greek.

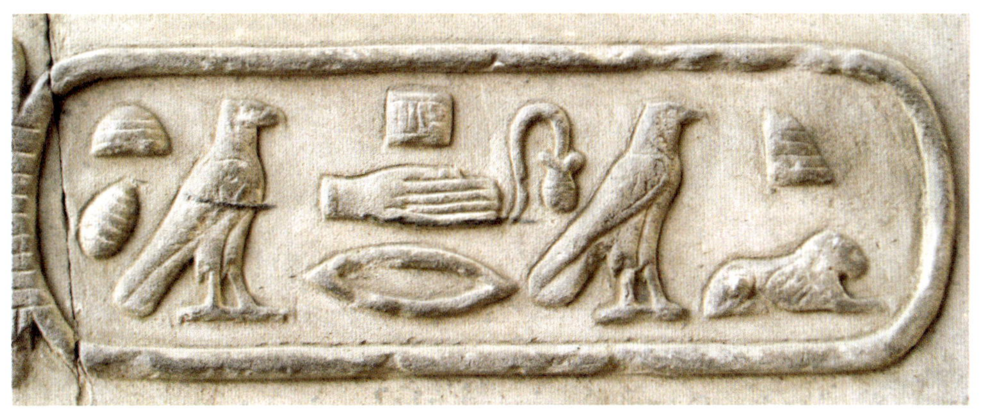

Cartouche in the Temple of Horus at Edfu. The inscribed name is Cleopatra.

Gods and Myths

The number of hieroglyphs connected to gods and their mythology is large. Ancient Egyptians believed their lives were merely a temporary state before their eternal afterlife among the gods. Furthermore, creation myths underpinned the existence of both the gods and the physical world. Venerating the numerous deities of the Egyptian pantheon, to ensure fertility and happiness, was part of daily ritual and was seen as a life-long preparation for the perilous journey to the afterlife.

The crossover between the names of gods and elements of nature (such as various animals and birds) that occur during interpretation of hieroglyphs mean that some symbols have several meanings. The next pages explore the deeper meaning of the deities to Egyptians, and symbols from the complex world of myth that evolved over more than 5000 years. Here we see Hathor wearing a headdress of cow horns and sun disk (opposite).

Hathor with the Pharaoh Menkaure, Fourth Dynasty.

The Eye of Horus

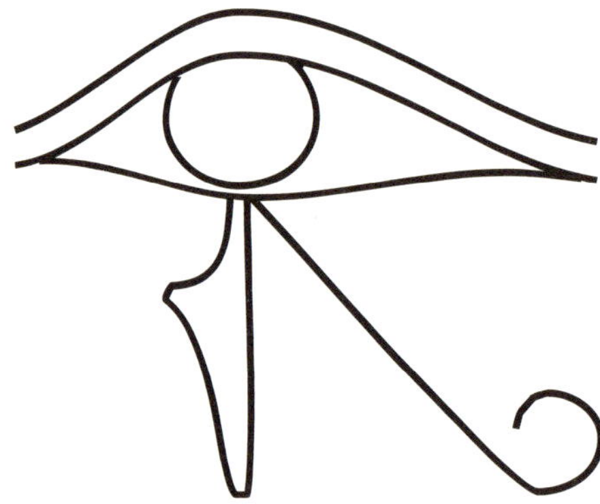

Symbol:

The Eye of Horus symbol, a stylized left eye with distinctive markings, was believed to have protective magical powers and appeared frequently in ancient Egyptian art. It was one of the most common motifs for amulets, and was in common use from the Old Kingdom (c. 2686–2181 BC) to the Roman period (30 BC – AD 64). The symbol was adopted by the people of regions neighbouring Egypt, especially to the south of Egypt in Nubian lands, as well as Syria and Canaan.

Meaning:

Also known as the wedjat eye, this falcon-inspired motif is a common image that brings a sense of wellbeing and safety to the observer. Representing healing and protection, its origins lie in the fabled conflict between the god Horus and his great rival Seth, the god of war. While fighting Seth Horus lost an eye, if not both of them – a major loss for the falcon god whose eyes represented the sun and moon. Horus eventually regained his eyes and with them the protective power they brought to Egypt.

The Eye of Ra

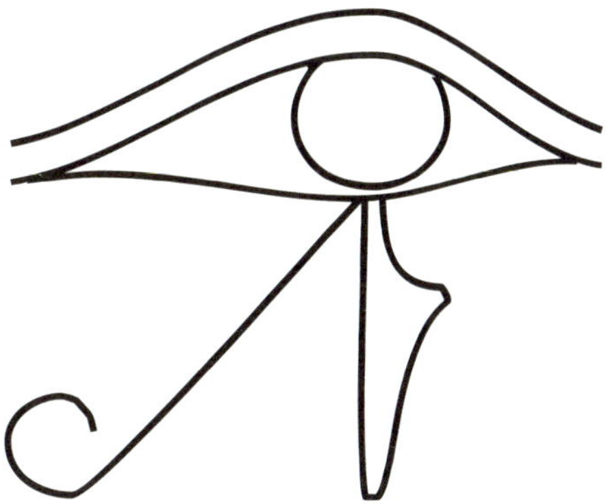

Symbol:

Visually the Eye of Ra is similar in style to the Eye of Horus, but its meaning and authority are quite different. This right eye came from Ra himself, ancient Egypt's god of the sun, whose life was linked to the beginning of the universe and all things in creation. Although the eye and god can exist independently in stories and art, they also come together to subjugate the enemies of Ra. The Eye of Ra was believed to possess a violent nature and destructive powers that drew strength from the sun itself.

Meaning:

The Eye was an extension of Ra's power, equated with the disk of the sun, and also operated as a goddess in its own right. Linked to or symbolizing several different deities, the Eye of Ra may be an extension of Hathor, Sekhmet, Bastet and Mut, among others. The glaring, violent aspect of the eye existed to defend Ra from any agents of disorder and chaos who sought to undermine his rule. In later traditions the Eye of Ra and the Eye of Horus were paired to represent the sun and moon respectively.

Osiris

Symbol:

The hieroglyph of Osiris shows the god wearing the Atef crown and is one of the many anthropomorphic gods in the hieroglyphic dictionary, most of whom can be distinguished only by their headdress. Here we see a combination of the Hedjet crown representing Upper Egypt and the feathers of an ostrich associated with the Osiris cult. As one of ancient Egypt's key deities, Osiris is represented in innumerable ways in art. His key role as god of the underworld stood alongside many roles as a god of fertility, resurrection and judgement in the afterlife.

Meaning:

One of the primary gods in the Egyptian pantheon, Osiris is known most widely as a god of death and the underworld. Osiris is the central point of the Egyptian pantheon – the oldest child of Geb (god of the earth) and Nut (goddess of the heavens. His younger siblings include Seth (god of war and chaos) and Isis (goddess of healing and rebirth). Osiris's life has a theme of kingship with his sister-wife Isis. Together they ruled Egypt through prosperous times and the many gifts of harvest and the flooding of the Nile were attributed to their wisdom. Motivated by jealousy, Osiris's brother Seth trapped him in a sealed coffin, which he cast into the Nile. Despite the efforts of Isis to save her husband, Osiris was never to return as pharaoh, destined to be lord of the afterlife forever.

The head of the god Osiris is here identified by the Atef crown and the uraeus (cobra) symbol he carried as king of the afterlife (600–550 BC).

Ankh

Symbol:

The ankh is a symbol whose power and familiarity has spread far beyond Egyptian history. This key of life symbol represented eternal life to the ancient Egyptians and was seen as the first true cross when it was adopted by the Coptic church.

The object most visually comparable to an *ankh* is the sandal strap. The word *ankh* also meant 'mirror' – items which were frequently found in tombs and used ceremonially in funerals.

Meaning:

Although the true origin of this amulet is unclear, it was very common for the *ankh* to be part of representations of gods and pharaohs, often being given and received between the two. They may also be held pointing towards people, as a 'breath of life'. Seen commonly in art and architecture of the pharaohs, this iconic shape was carried and worn as a reminder and talisman during one's time on earth.

Ankhs were also placed in the sarcophagus or tomb to bring good luck for the journey to the afterlife and beyond. The *ankh* was a symbol for all. Its continuing popularity today suggests that the human need for good luck charms is still alive.

Tyet

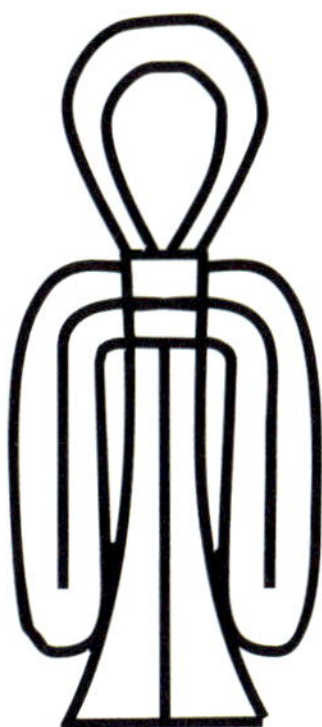

Symbol:

This symbol, in hieroglyphic form, represents the amulet shape known by some as the *tyet* (or *tit*). It is also known as the knot (or girdle) of Isis and resembles a knotted piece of cloth that is pointed (or hanging) down. This symbol has been found in burial sites from the beginnings of the New Kingdom, when such items became popular and were often found in mummy wrappings. In construction, it is similar to the more familiar shape of the *ankh*.

Meaning:

Its association with the goddess Isis meant it was venerated throughout Egyptian society. As the Mother Goddess of the universe, Isis held many roles and was associated with all the major gods. She was the sister-wife of Osiris and mother of Horus. She held magical powers of protection and was prayed to in times of illness or troubles in the family. The *tyet* amulet enabled all to carry her luck and protection with them. Isis, as a universal mother, was the goddess most linked to reproduction and the symbol of folded cloth is thought to refer to the use of such material during the menstrual cycle.

Shu

Symbol:

Shu is the god of both air and sunlight, and is most often identified by the tall feather worn on his head. He is one of the nine primary deities created by the Heliopolis priests in what is called the Great Ennead and given life by the solar god, and father of this group, Atum. The birth of this group appears in the Pyramid Texts, with the main gods of creation including the central sun god Ra.

Meaning:

The name Shu may also mean 'emptiness' as he is the personification of air, and his body is made of fog and clouds, according to the Pyramid Texts. The story of a king's ascent to the heavens after death speaks of his journey via the bones of Shu. In Egyptian art, Shu is often portrayed holding his daughters between himself and the sky. Nut, the sky goddess, is his daughter and Geb, the earth god, is his son.

Occasionally Shu was depicted in the form of a lion or as a lion-headed man. Sculptures of Shu are few and, like other art, are mostly from the New Kingdom period. His most famous artefact shows Shu holding aloft the ivory headrest found in the tomb of Tutankhamun, with lions as guards on each side.

The god of the air and supporter of the sky, Shu, adorned by a feather, seen here beneath the goddess of the cosmos, Nut, depicted as the night sky and stars.

Sobek

Symbol:

The crocodile was an animal that inspired terror in Egyptian life and respect for this huge beast fed into its depiction. The crocodile-alone hieroglyph shares meanings such as greedy, anger and voracious.

Sobek is a god whose image is based around the crocodile, both whole and as a crocodile-headed human. A protector god with the strength of the Nile crocodile, he could fight and kill for both good and ill. Sobek's symbol shows a whole Nile crocodile atop a holy chest, proving his divine nature. Despite the fear Sobek was a popular god, connected to water and fertility and most commonly worshipped in the area of the vast Fayum lake.

Meaning:

Sobek became more important over the dynasties. The crocodile god was a fertility figure of great brutality and kindness who ensured the banks of the Nile and the land of Egypt's north were green and fertile. Because he was the god of water (the Nile itself was believed to flow from his sweat), the many dynasties of ancient Egypt felt it was important to have Sobek by the pharaoh's side. His regular representation in temples and tombs shows how greatly he was revered. Sobek was feared because of his ability to create chaos if upset as well as being admired as early Egyptians also believed he brought order to the world. It was thought he had created the Nile valley. Sadly there are no crocodiles north of the Aswan Dam today, but for visitors to Egypt the temple of Kom Ombo, north of Aswan and built in the Graeco–Roman period, is a fascinating stop. It's believed the mummified crocodiles you can see there were raised there.

The crocodile god Sobek carved in the Temple of Kom Ombo by the Nile in Upper Egypt. This temple is known as 'the crocodile temple' or 'the domain of Sobek'.

Scarab (Dung) Beetle

Symbol:
Recreated in art, jewellery and writings, the dung beetle represented both hard work and the endless cycle of regeneration. Its success as an insect made it a symbol of life which inspired early Egyptians. The sight of the beetle continuously rolling its eggs in dung balls, from which new beetles appeared, symbolized the daily solar cycle. The scarab in amulets or on royal seals was therefore shown pushing (or rolling) the sun, rather than a dung ball.

Meaning:
Revered as a worker of tireless effort and linking the cycle of the sun to the human cycles of life and regeneration, the scarab beetle is a central member of the cast of pharaonic Egypt's most recognizable symbols. The use of the scarab in a multitude of artefacts illustrates the warmth and esteem in which the beetle's work was held. It is not unusual to find the beetle's shape mixed with other creatures, such as birds of prey, by the addition of wings or other features. Linked with all gods and pharaohs in the art of temples, tombs and buildings, the scarab is most associated with Khepri, whose name was the sound of the hieroglyph for the beetle as spoken.

Neith Emblem

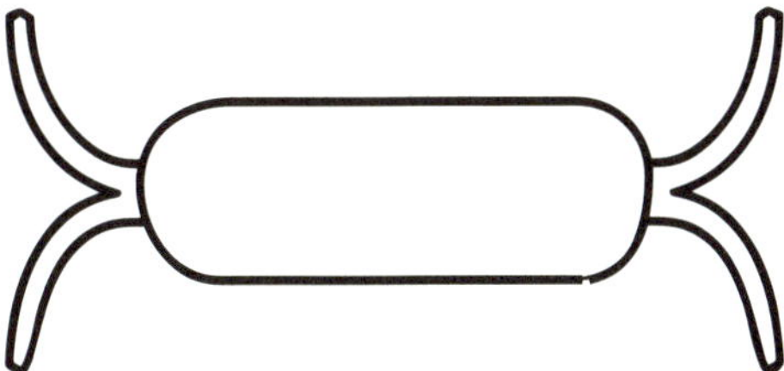

Symbol:

From early civilizations onwards the bow was the most dangerous and commonly used weapon. Hieroglyphs are evidence of their importance, with multiple variants of this symbol. Arrowheads over 60,000 years old have been discovered in southern Africa. In Egypt, an early deity linked to warfare and hunting was the goddess Neith, with this representation of crossed bows one her earliest symbols. As the technology and use of the bow developed, symbols and art changed too. Egypt's kings used the bow to represent the enemy when shown with captured foreign fighters.

Meaning:

Neith was worshipped as a goddess from Egypt's prehistory to the demise of the pharaohs. While she was named 'mistress of the bow' or 'ruler of arrows', she was also associated with creation and funerary beliefs and, because her cult centre was in the Egyptian Delta at Sais, she was also goddess of Lower Egypt. Little remains of Sais today; its main period of influence was during the 24th and 26th Dynasties when it was capital of the country. When Jean-François Champollion (who deciphered the Rosetta Stone and opened hieroglyphs to the world) visited in the 19th century, he felt that the visible mud walls of the city were part of the temple of Neith.

Anubis

Symbol:

Anubis is Egypt's foremost canine god. His name can be found on the walls of Egypt's oldest burial grounds and he is referenced in prayers as a protector god of the dead. In hieroglyphs this canine god is best known when seen lying on a wooden chest, though the dog appears in a variety of symbols representing other gods.

Although Anubis is assumed to be a jackal, it is unclear whether his shape is a wild dog, a wolf, a fox or a jackal. Anubis is represented in all ancient Egyptian art forms, including sculpture, on mummies, tomb paintings, temple walls and papyrus. Other major deities that can assume a jackal- or wolf-like shape include Seth and Wepwawet, who are associated with chaos, turmoil and rage.

Meaning:

A central figure to ancient Egypt's afterlife, Anubis was the key deity linked to embalming, mummification and the use of canopic jars. Anubis was pre-eminent as god of the dead for centuries before the rise of Osiris.

In his fully dog form Anubis was a dark figure, imagined as
'keeper of the secrets'. Anubis's role added an air of mystery to
the work of temple priests. Associated with many gods from
the Old Kingdom onwards, Anubis was ultimately assimilated
into the broad cult of Osiris, who then became known as his
father. Other gods had claimed Anubis as their own offspring,
including Bastet, Seth and Ra. This role as mediator between
life and afterlife ensured recognition in the tombs of many
pharaohs, where Anubis is often portrayed as a jackal-headed
human. Anubis was venerated long into Graeco–Roman times.

*The god Anubis sculpted in his classic position as protector of the dead in this late-period piece,
664–30 BC.*

Bastet

Symbol:

The cat goddess Bastet is not portrayed as a hieroglyph in cat form, but linked instead to the hieroglyph showing an ointment jar, which may have either medicinal or burial use. Cats were often carved onto the tops of such jars or depicted on them. The goddess Bastet defended the family from diseases and evil spirits, in particular illnesses affecting women and children. The cat hieroglyph shows a domestic cat in outline, and is pronounced 'miu'.

Meaning:

The ancient Egyptians are thought to have been the first civilization to domesticate cats, a relationship that continues to thrive today. Cats were seen as wild animals in early Egypt, however. Cats were manifested in sacred form from pre-dynastic times and appear throughout Egypt's story. They were initially seen as a lioness-headed woman on early stone vessels as early as the Second Dynasty. From her home cult city of Bubastis, Bastet's popularity grew steadily across ancient Egypt. Her depiction as a fierce lioness softened to more domesticated cat-like representation.

As a feline-headed woman, Bastet was thought to bring family
harmony to the homes of Egyptians when they themselves
had accepted the domesticated cat. She was the daughter of
the sun god Ra and revered in many roles, among them as
goddess of the East, love, intoxication, music and dance, joy
and celebration. At the height of her popularity the annual
Bastet festival was one of Egypt's largest events, marked by wild
drinking and dancing.

*The cat goddess Bastet sitting behind a king who is wearing the double crown. Bastet was often sculpted
and painted wearing a dress and necklace, as visible here. Temple of Haroeris, Kom Ombo.*

Serket

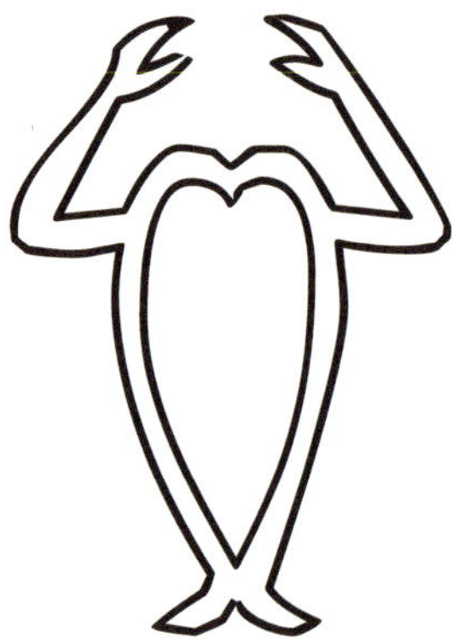

Symbol:

This depiction of a scorpion is a stylized hieroglyph used to represent the goddess Serket, and is pronounced as such. This symbol was a deliberately reduced and stylized shape due to the fearsome reputation of the real living creature. Because it was depicted without the threatening tail and the fearsome head, the goddess was believed to take on an impotent form of its dangerous self. This made Serket acceptable to the living when shown in funeral chapels as a deity who guarded the dead.

Meaning:

The scorpion was a danger that existed in ancient Egypt's daily life, associated with hiding in the shadows and appearing on walls and ceilings, threatening attack. A separate hieroglyph of the scorpion as a natural shape exists and is pronounced *serk*. The goddess Serket was seen as a protector of the dead alongside Isis, Neith and Nephthys. When depicted on the sarcophagus of a dead pharaoh, or as an amulet in the tomb, Serket could be seen as a scorpion with a woman's head (or the reverse). Serket was important to pharaohs for her power to protect them from deadly scorpion stings. Such powers to preserve life were also called upon by rulers for wider protection during battles or disasters. A goddess of long-standing, she was called Serket-betu, meaning 'the one who brings breath to the throat', a reference to her powers to protect life.

Carving of the goddess of magic Serqet shown with a scorpion on her head.
Interior wall of the Temple of Horus, Edfu.

Sa

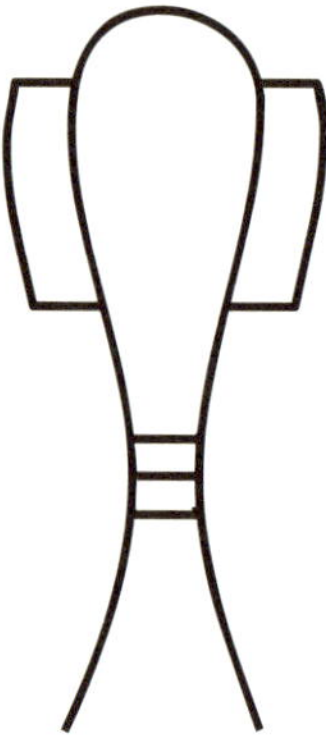

Symbol:

A symbol of protection, *sa* is represented by a rolled-up mat
made from papyrus reeds. Believed to have been used by
herdsman for sleep or shelter, it may also have been an early
form of life-preserver used by Nile boatmen. As a symbol of
protection it was commonplace on amulets and in jewellery
such as necklaces. It is often held in the hands of gods in
statuary, particularly linked to the god Tawaret, a goddess of
great popularity throughout Egyptian society.

Meaning:

Sa stood for 'protection' and was grouped with other
hieroglyphs to represent the terms 'bodyguard' or 'attendant'.
The *sa* symbol itself was found in art from the Old Kingdom
onwards, and over time became associated with such symbols
as the *ankh* and *was* sceptre. Its association with Bes, who
guarded against snake bites and protected pregnant women,
and the hippopotamus goddess of childbirth Tawaret, grew over
time. The *sa* hieroglyph is therefore widely found on artefacts
from the New Kingdom. Ancient Egyptians' preoccupation
with resurrection and reaching the afterlife ensured protective
symbols were popular in all strata of society. *Sa* was also
depicted on objects linked to magical powers as a guard against
evil spirits.

Heh

Symbol:

This hieroglyph of the god Heh shows him supporting the sky. The name is pronounced as 'hey'. Heh was one of the eight primeval gods of the Ogdoad existing before the creation of the world. Heh represented infinity. Because of this the Heh hieroglyph also means 'million' and 'many'. Over time Heh came to also represent the spirit of eternity.

Meaning:

Heh is an important symbol. The Egyptians' belief in eternity was central to their daily and religious life. Heh was not associated with any one place or period, but rather was venerated by all Egyptians individually and was depicted widely within stories of gods and pharaohs. He was most often shown in painted form kneeling and holding a notched palm branch in each hand. These branches were created to measure time (the hieroglyph M4 illustrates this). When shown in the hands of Heh they indicate infinity. Heh was usually paired with Hauhet, a female deity also linked to idea of an eternal afterlife.

Thoth

Symbol:

One of Egypt's main deities, references to Thoth in the Old
Kingdom show his central position as god of the moon and
worldly wisdom. As shown here, Thoth could be represented
in human form with an ibis head, but also as a sitting baboon.
Like other gods, whose importance continued through ancient
Egypt's story, Thoth's story became interwoven with other gods
and he was portrayed as a protector of the universe, attending
the weighing of the heart ceremony. Despite this fluidity of
image, Thoth retained his position as the deity of knowledge,
a role key enough that he was eventually assimilated into the
Greek god Hermes.

Meaning:

One of the eight primordial deities who formed the Ogdoad
of Hermopolis, Thoth played many roles in Egyptian
mythology. His connections to the cycle of the moon and role
in maintaining the universe linked his name to a wide range of
responsibilities. Thoth was heavily associated with the magical
arts, oversaw the writing system and was involved in judging
the dead. His consort was the goddess Maat.

Usually shown with an ibis head, with the moon above, Thoth
was the reason the ibis was so revered in ancient Egypt.
In a land ruled by the regular rise and fall of the Nile,

measurement was important to ancient Egyptians, touching all areas of daily life. Thoth oversaw measurement and it was in this role he was represented as a baboon. Thoth hieroglyphs were used at ceremonies involving time and weight, as well as being employed as guards to the underworld. The association between Thoth and the ibis and baboon led to the revering of these creatures and their mummification in vast numbers. The cult centre of Tuna el-Gebel, near Hermopolis, has an underground network of tombs filled with these creatures, and at Saqqara a necropolis of 4 million birds is to be found.

The god of the moon, science, knowledge and many things, Thoth is here shown in the Valley of the Nobles. His Egyptian name was Djehuty, 'He who is like an Ibis'.

Afterlife

The challenges of safely reaching the afterlife were expressed in specific myths and hieroglyphs, not least in texts such as the Coffin Texts and Pyramid Texts, which made up a significant proportion of the writings we now know as the Book of the Dead. These spells of protection found on artefacts, tomb walls and mummy wrappings form perhaps the most valuable source for those studying hieroglyphs and ancient Egypt.

In this section we look at rituals and beliefs linked to life in the world of the *Duat*, a place where gods such as Osiris, Anubis and the goddess Maat may be encountered on the way to a land Egyptians believed was green and verdant and rewarded them for their faith while they were in the land of the living.

The tomb of Seti I in the Valley of the Kings is a vast complex. The burial chamber ceiling is covered in astronomical decorations that show constellations and annual calendars of the cosmos.

Seba

Symbol:

The stars were a source of constant fascination and study in ancient Egypt. The religious significance of the daily cycle of day and night meant it was the priests alone who developed the science of astronomy. The need to understand the movements of celestial bodies was essential in ancient Egypt in order to understand and predict the seasons. This affected farming, festivals, the weather and, most of all, helped indicate the arrival of the Nile's annual inundation. Intricate ongoing observation and recording of the cosmos over millennia ensured that ancient Egypt's astronomical records were one of its greatest scientific gifts to the world.

Meaning:

It is clear from the art decorating the ceilings of many tombs and in writings featuring stars that centuries of observation led to accurate knowledge of the night sky. Representions of the night stars and many constellations had been identified in ancient times, and this five-pointed symbol is also connected to religion and the afterlife. Those tombs today that are still adorned with dark blue ceilings covered in yellow *seba* shapes give visitors the clearest sense of the relationship and transition between the dead of the sarcophagus and the universe above.

Ceilings of temples in ancient Egypt were adorned with stars because these buildings were intended to be models of the cosmos in miniature. Within such intricately decorated spaces the living world, skies and the realm of the dead (*Duat*) all coexisted to reflect Egyptians' belief in immortality. There are many beautiful and intricate paintings of the skies in ancient Egypt's monuments, including the magnificent representation of astronomical and astrological vision in the Temple of Hathor at Dendera and the vividly coloured tomb of Ramses VI.

Part of the magnificent astronomical ceiling of the Temple of Hathor at Dendera, featuring the Eye of Horus and the god Thoth.

Ba

Symbol:

The *ba* and the *ka*, or spirit, were believed to represent the two parts of the human soul. The *ba* was the soul itself and in hieroglyphs is represented as a bird with a human head – and sometimes arms. The *ba* accompanied people through life and beyond and was frequently referred to in the writings of ancient Egypt. This soul was also given physical form in wooden bird statuettes found in burials in the late Ptolemaic period. They were attached to a coffin or other forms of funerary ornaments.

Meaning:

Until the end of the Old Kingdom being associated with one's *ba* was a gift only for the gods and kings of Heliopolis and Memphis. From that point it became more usual for all Egyptians to be aware of their living soul and to nurture it through life. This ensured they would live a good life and be filled with wisdom when they passed into the afterlife. A prayer for the dead stated 'Come forth as the living Ba, see the sun disk at dawn, come and go to the sacred cemetery.'

The *ba* in bird form represents the mobility of the soul after death as it flies to heaven in search of a new life. In tombs the *ba* is seen as a human-headed bird leaving the deceased. The bird's face is a painted likeness of the dead person in life.

Carved images of the soul (ba) of Osiris in the form of human-headed birds decorate the eastern Osiris chapels of Dendera, Temple of Hathor.

Duat

Symbol:

The *Duat* is one of a sequence of star-based symbols in the hieroglyphic dictionary. In this case, rather than being associated with the sky seen by the living, it is a symbol of the skies of the underworld (or more accurately called the 'otherworld'), which was itself named *Duat*. This world was a place through which the dead travelled, and where the sun went during the hours of darkness. Within it dwelt many gods whose role was to maintain the continuity of the world, including Maat overseeing the weighing of the heart ceremony for those arriving there after dying.

Meaning:

This beautiful star-like image connected earthly life in ancient Egypt with the otherworld. It was believed that stars did not just exist in the skies of the mortal world, but also in the *Duat*, the realm of the dead, through which the sun travelled on its nightly journey. Gods such as Osiris, Re, Anubis, Thoth, Hathor and Horus lived alongside Maat in the *Duat*. This was the world the dead passed through by undertaking a series of tests in order to find *Aaru*, a world for evermore filled with an abundance of food where they would live eternally.

Here two baboons offer the Wedjat eye to the sun god Khepri (as a beetle),
who is holding the symbol for Duat, *the underworld.*

Maat Feather

Symbol:

Most commonly, this symbol is seen as connected to the goddess Maat, a central figure in Egyptian religion. She was responsible for upholding values such as harmony, truth and fairness both in human life and among the gods. Maat ensured that Egypt's people followed a strict code of ethics, a code upheld by the pharaoh as proof of their adherence to cosmic law. Maat was also a deity of such import that the sun's first hour of each day was represented by this goddess.

Meaning:

Maat oversaw the weighing of the heart ceremony. As the personification of truth and justice in society, it was she against whom the heart was weighed. This tribunal was held at the end of life according to the myths of ancient Egypt. The heart of each person was weighed against Maat's feather – which is usually depicted in her headdress – to judge their right to live in the afterlife. Its lightness ensured that those being judged passed safely into the next world.

Ka

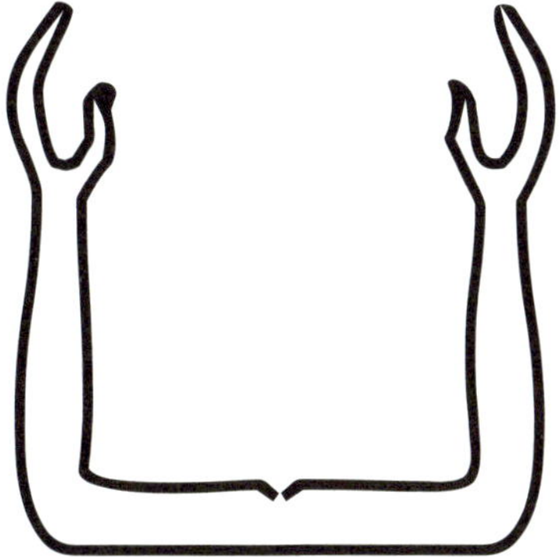

Symbol:

The *ka*, along with the *ba* and the *akh* in ancient Egyptian religion, represent the key aspects of the soul of both humans and gods. The hieroglyph is written as two raised arms and was a common symbol of the writing system from its earliest development. The two raised arms symbolised a defensive position to ward away negative powers that may reduce energy in the living. It is often paired with hieroglyphs related to work, building and food.

Meaning:

The *ka* is an element of human life which arrives with birth and continues to, and beyond, death. The *ka* passes from parent to child but is shaped by the god Khnum, who creates the body before birth. This was done on a potters wheel, determining the child's physical and spiritual being. Beyond life, the *ka* still required sustenance and therefore food was offered to the deceased in tombs, both in offerings and depicted as decoration. In Early Dynastic periods, the raised arms can be seen shaped as though carrying a plate offering food.

Mummy

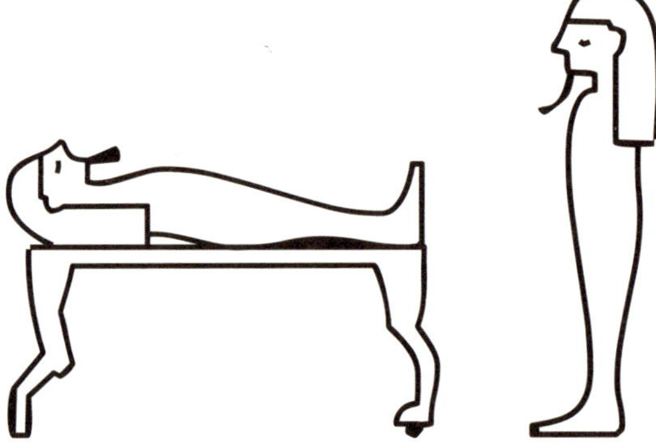

Symbol:

Few things in popular consciousness are more representative of ancient Egypt than mummies. Not surprisingly, there are several hieroglyphs that use the mummy as a symbol. Here we see two of them – first, a prone mummy representing death and the corpse, but also sleep. An upright mummy is associated with the stage before burial, when the body was prepared. This hieroglyph was first being seen around the 12th Dynasty, some time after mummification was common.

Meaning:

The association between sleep and lying on a funeral bed was close in the Egyptian mind, whether in the world of dreams or being prepared for burial and the afterlife. One needed protection from the gods, who kept away evil at night, a time of chaos and when demons might attack under cover of dark.

The upright mummy, bound in linen and wearing the familiar wig and beard, is a shape seen most often in death amulets called *ushabti* or 'the answerer'. These items made sure the body was ready to be called to work again if required. *Ushabti* are small versions of mummies, just few centimetres long, which were found wrapped in mummy cloth and scattered in tombs. These represented the human's life and came decorated to different degrees, perhaps holding tools to reflect the life and work of the deceased. As many as 365 have been found in a single tomb, protecting the dead all year round.

Ushabti from the tomb of Tutankhamum. Such figures were often found inside mummy wrappings or spread in tombs in multiple quantities, to help the deceased's journey.

Ib

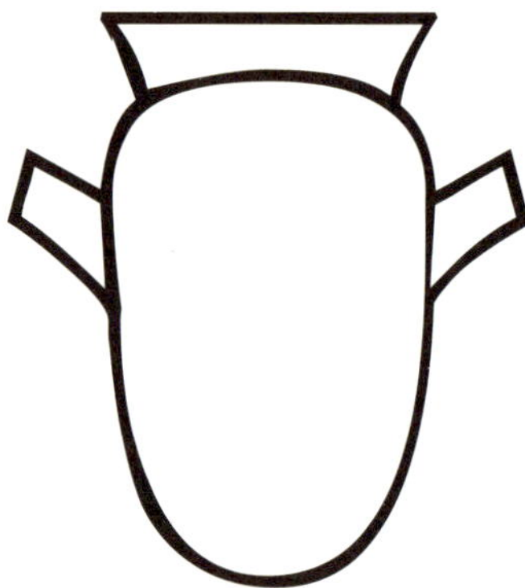

Symbol:

The heart was, literally, the centre of many aspects of life and death to Egyptians. As well as providing life by creating the pulse, it was known as the seat of intelligence in all animals, and for humans the centre of their religious beliefs. It was also important as the source of joy and happiness, and this positive association led to the heart hieroglyph being included in messages of love and friendship after death. These would be on jewellery or jars buried in tombs. The heart held a special place in Egyptian religion as it was believed that the creation god Ptah brought forth the universe having made it in his own heart.

Meaning:

The heart hieroglyph appears as a combination of the organ itself and as a type of container. This signified that the heart held life itself and should be kept safe. Ancient Egyptians believed that the heart's condition affected many aspects of human behaviour, including mood and the ability to work with physical energy and strong will. The heart's role as container of both soul and intelligence meant that it was the only organ left in the body during mummification. When a person died and faced judgement to enter the afterlife, it was the heart that was weighed on scales held by the goddess Maat.

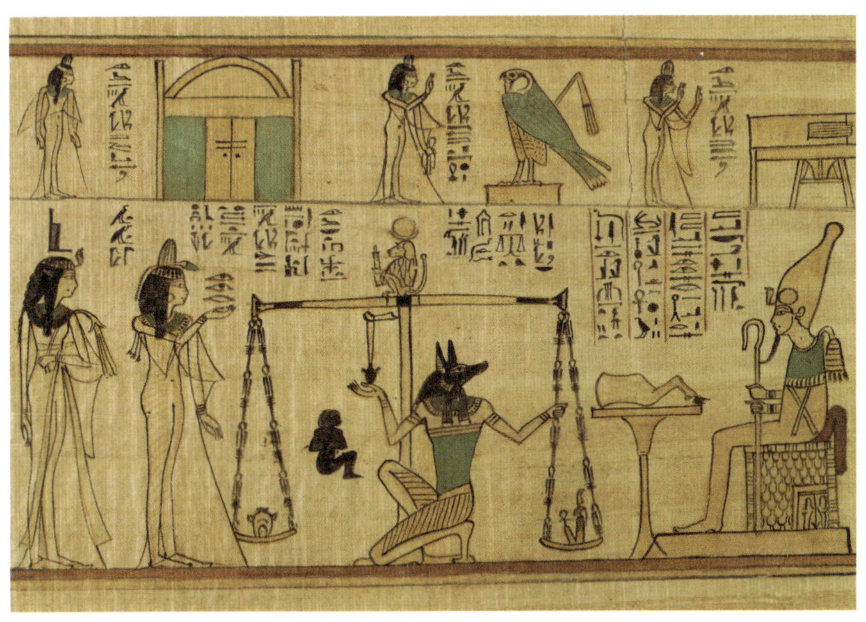

The weighing of the heart ceremony was spell 125 in the papyrus that accompanied Nauny, a chantress of the god Amun-Re, as part of her funerary equipment. She died c. 1050 BC.

Offering Table

Symbol:

This hieroglyph is a symbol from the wide range of hieroglyphs relating to the process that linked death to a successful journey to the afterlife. The offering table represented idealizes a place where, at the time of burial and perhaps for many years to come, relatives would deliver gifts to sustain and protect the dead in their 'house of eternity'. Offering tables could be inscribed with the text beginning 'An offering which the king grants...' followed by names of the gods to be fed and a list of food and drink. The deceased's family may have visited the tomb regularly, where the typical offering space could be a reed mat rather than a table. It was also possible for proxy visitors to be sent by those unable to visit themselves.

Meaning:

In temples or for wealthier Egyptians an actual table would be in place and, in order to maintain the support of the deceased each day, offering tables were often carved with images of typical offerings of foods – these may include such items as bread, beer, meat and other staples. Reciting the 'offering formula' could also substitute for a real offering. This formula allowed the deceased to enjoy the offerings by reciting from stelae or other tomb objects their thanks in the name of a king to receive such gifts. The deceased's name would be carved or painted into the offering before the closing of the tomb.

Bas-relief from the tomb of Ra-hetep, a priest of Memphis, showing him seated before a table of offerings. From Meydum, Fourth Dynasty.

Key Discoveries

The rich evidence left behind from ancient Egypt is frequently added to, with significant discoveries being made, it seems, almost daily. Many archaeologists also feel that a vast archive remains buried and undiscovered.

The story of the decipherment and understanding of Egypt's chronology, however, has been underpinned by the discovery of artefacts with hieroglyphs, which have provided the stepping stones to a more complete picture of ancient Egyptian life and culture. Several key objects are explained in this section, with their role in our understanding of the past.

A bust of Jean-François Champollion, the scholar who deciphered the Rosetta Stone,
on display in the Egyptian Museum Cairo.

The Narmer Palette

Symbol:

The Narmer Palette, which is also known as the Great Hierakonpolis Palette, dates from c. 3200–3000 BC and is significant for featuring some of the earliest hieroglyphs found in Egypt. Carved from a single piece of siltstone, it is believed to have been used for ceremonial purposes. It depicts the First Dynasty king Narmer uniting Upper and Lower Egypt as he vanquishes his enemies on the battlefield. Familiar hieroglyphs such as the strong bull and Horus figures appear, along with the flail image and red crown and a multitude of small animal and god symbols.

Meaning:

The Narmer Palette has been the subject of many theories and interpretations since its discovery in 1897 at the Temple of Horus in Nekhen, by James Quibell and Frederick Green.

King Narmer was a pharaoh of the Early Dynastic Period and is widely regarded as the founder of the First Dynasty and unifier of Upper and Lower Egypt. Confusingly, Narmer is also thought to be known as Menes; their serekhs (rectangular name boxes which predated the cartouche) have a startling similarity. King Narmer's name was spelt with a combination of two ideograms, the catfish (*Nar*) and the chisel (*Mer*).

The Narmer Palette is a ground-breaking object for many reasons, being some of the earliest evidence of the styles of pharaonic clothing and ornament that became familiar subsequently. The false royal beard (called a postiche and made of metal), which all rulers were shown with thereafter, makes its first appearance here, in both depictions of the king. Significantly Narmer was the first king to be portrayed wearing both the red and white crowns of Egypt, as its unifying king. Narmer is also shown wearing the *shendyt*. This garment was a type of loincloth, similar to a modern kilt, that was typically

worn by Egypt's ruling class. This piece of clothing, and the
more ornate sandals worn by Narmer to protect him on his
travels into the afterlife, became standard representations of
kings for centuries to come. Narmer is depicted as a skilled
warrior on the battlefield and was known as a master tactician,
always ready to fight and kill without mercy. On the palette,
beheaded men are part of his victory procession. Variants of the
meaning of Narmer's name in hieroglyphs were 'Fierce Catfish
of Horus' and 'Manly Catfish of Horus'. However, when he was
known as Menes, his name was 'He Who Endures'.

The Narmer Palette is one of the first major historical records of Egypt. The victorious King Narmer
is shown wearing both the crowns of Upper and Lower Egypt, the first king of both lands.

The Abydos King List

Symbol:

On the wall of the temple of Seti I at Abydos there is a carving showing the names and cartouches of 76 Egyptian kings. Dating from c. 1250 BC, the list covers much of the period between the First and 18th Dynasties. It has been invaluable to Egyptologists, filling in gaps in our knowledge and helping to reconstruct the pharaonic timeline and the names of kings. Its help in identifying kings in the Seventh and Eighth Dynasties has been of particular value, and the cartouches themselves are a treasure trove of hieroglyphs for those wishing to read and interpret this sacred language.

Meaning:

The creation of a king list was one way that pharaohs honoured their predecessors while reinforcing their authority as a ruler. The Abydos List is the best-known one found; none are complete. The *History of Egypt (Aegyptiaca)*, written in Greek by an Egyptian priest named Manetho from Heliopolis in the third century BC, was the first actual text to divide Egypt's history into 30 dynasties.

The king list in Abydos is a chronology of cartouches, starting with Narmer (Menes) at the top-left as you look at the wall. It ends with the builder of the temple, Menmaatre (Seti I) on the right side, lower down. All the kings face to their left, above their cartouche. Such a list was one way a living king could invoke the spirits of their favoured ancestors. The ruler of Egypt was a divine descendent of the gods in the eyes of the people, their role passed to them from their father (or mother). Therefore, their lineage was vital to their legitimacy as king. The omissions from the list also tell a story. The 'heretic' Amarna kings were excluded entirely, along with four kings from the 11th Dynasty and all in the Second Intermediate Period.

*Cartouches from the Abydos King List, situated off the second hypostyle hall
of the Great Temple of Abydos.*

Book of the Dead

Symbol:

The Egyptian Books of the Dead are best known as scrolls filled with spells to guide the owner through their journey through death to the afterlife, as protection for their mummified bodies. One of the best known is the Papyrus of Ani, written in Thebes c. 1250 BC, shown here. The scrolls are more correctly called *The Book of Going Forth by Day*, and were illustrated with hieroglyphs and painted scenes of life and the afterlife, similar to the finest tomb paintings. The texts included spells, declarations in preparation for the journey ahead and praise of the gods. This magnificent papyrus was prepared by the royal scribe Ani and two others. Ani held the title of 'Royal scribe veritable, scribe and accountant of the divine offerings'.

Meaning:

The scrolls that we know collectively as the 'Books of the Dead' are collections of spells that had a long history of use before they were set down, and illustrated, on papyrus. These spells were inscribed on coffins, sarcophagi and objects, as well as being painted on tomb walls. They were intended for the deceased to chant in their tomb as a way to connect with Osiris, god of the dead, and find their way into the afterlife.

During the New Kingdom these spells began appearing on mummy wrappings, on papyrus scrolls and in the coffins of a wider range of society, having been reserved for royalty and the privileged for millennia. Spells from the Book of the Dead have been found in tombs across Egyptian history, with two particular periods providing much of our knowledge. First, the spells known as the Pyramid Texts, found at Saqqara and dating from the Old Kingdom, provided insight into how the first rulers were buried and protected in death. Second, groups of spells (partly derived from the Pyramid Texts) and dated c. 2100 BC were found buried with mummies from all strata of Egyptian society. These are known as the Coffin Texts. The

spells are written both in hieroglyphic and hieratic scripts
and focus on the dangers to be confronted in the *Duat*, the
underground world ruled by Osiris. Over 1000 spells of varying
lengths have been found from the Middle Kingdom, some of
which were adopted and adapted before inclusion in the Book
of the Dead scrolls of the New Kingdom. The use of this type
of spell became more individual over time. The use of linen
as a material to wrap the body made it possible to add words
to the fabric, which allowed extra protection by adding direct
contact with the skin. Scroll writing was the highest form of
art to record the words and images that protected the deceased
pharaoh or powerful member of society. The inclusion of spells
in burials lasted into the Ptolemaic era (305–30 BC), when
Egypt came under Greek rule. The translation of the Books of
the Dead has been key to understanding the relationship of
Egyptian civilization with its religion. The detailed hieroglyphs
help us look back on this long-lived civilization with the
knowledge that people spent each day awaiting a journey to the
eternal afterlife that was based on their earthly life story and
successfully facing the tests they faced with the gods of eternity.

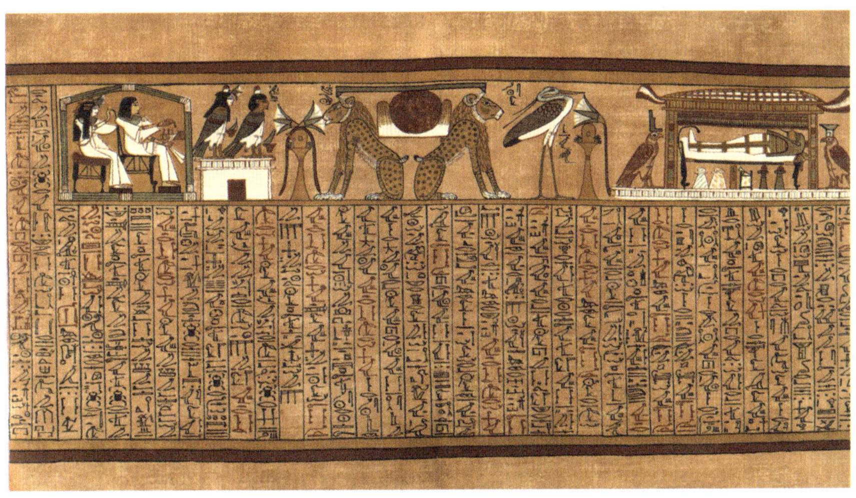

*Illustration from the Papyrus of Ani, a papyrus manuscript in the form of a scroll with cursive hieroglyphs
that was created c. 1250 BC, during the 19th Dynasty of the New Kingdom.*

Rosetta Stone

The discovery of the Rosetta Stone in 1799 by Pierre-François Bouchard paved the way to finally deciphering the ancient Egyptian language. The discovery of an object that was written in three different scripts (hieroglyphs, demotic and ancient Greek) led to great excitement as it was quickly realized that the stone held the key to deciphering the previously locked language of hieroglyphs. The stone was found in the Nile Delta near the town of Rashid (Rosetta), during Napoleon's Egyptian campaign. The text itself is a decree issued on behalf of King Ptolemy V Epiphanes, ruler of Egypt from 204 BC.

It was in 1822 that Jean-François Champollion announced, in Paris, the transliteration of the hieroglyphic texts. From that point scholars began work on their understanding of the huge number of different hieroglyphic symbols found throughout Egypt. It is true to say that this single discovery led to the modern world understanding the story of Egyptian civilization.

Meaning:

The deciphering of the Rosetta Stone was to prove a complex challenge. The use of hieroglyphs in Egypt had stopped over 1400 years before its discovery and the use of demotic language had ended not much later, rendering the ancient Egyptian language obsolete for centuries. The discovery of the stone triggered an academic scrabble of scholars wishing to be the first to decipher its text and finally unlock the mysteries of ancient Egypt. However, its challenges were such that only two people managed to stay the course – Champollion, who was to prove himself the winner, was a French philologist with a devotion to the idea of unlocking the truths about Egyptian civilization, and his competitor Thomas Young. Young was a British physicist for whom the challenge of decipherment was like that of a giant logic puzzle. Young showed little interest in Egypt itself, but enjoyed the race to be first against a French rival at a time when the two nations were in competition on the world stage. The two followed differing paths in their work, with Young's focused on his assumption that hieroglyphs did not represent sounds, whereas Champollion took the advantage of his own knowledge of the Coptic language to gamble on the idea that Coptic, a language only used in the churches of the time, had its foundation in ancient Egypt's language. In 1822 Champollion looked at other examples of hieroglyphs, including a cartouche from Abu Simbel. Logic suggested the symbols must represent the name Rameses, due to the repetition of the letter 's'. This moment provided important verification of Champollion's belief that hieroglyphs represented a phonetic Egyptian language.

The Rosetta Stone, discovered during Napoleon's Egyptian expedition, allowed decipherment of hieroglyphs. It features hieroglyphs, demotic script and Greek text of the same decree for comparison.

Sarcophagus of Khonsu

The village of Deir el-Medina is a short stop for most visitors on their whirlwind trip around Luxor's west bank. The mud brick remains give little indication of the major role the tight-knit and expert community who lived there played in creating the burial sites of New Kingdom pharaohs and other important figures. Skilled artisans in all mediums lived here for some 400 years and furnished and decorated walls, coffins and objects with art and hieroglyphs. Such was the importance of their work that, over time, they became artists and craftsmen of high value, stature and wealth in their own right. Much of the art a visitor now finds in the tombs of the Valleys of Queens and Kings was painted by the denizens of Deir el-Medina, who termed themselves 'servants in the Place of Truth'. Those who gained high standing in Deir el-Medina deserved their own recognition in the afterlife, making beautifully decorated coffins for their own journeys after death.

This sarcophagus was discovered by the great French Egyptologist Gaston Maspero in 1886. The tomb he entered near the village contained 20 bodies, many perfectly preserved within coffins, including Khonsu. The art which surrounds the box has many of the hallmarks of the work of the artisans employed in the famous tombs of Egypt's rulers. It must surely be true that the hieroglyphs, art and gods who protected kings and queens when they left the earth must shelter these workers, too.

The sarcophagus for Khonsu's journey to the afterlife was mostly protected by spells taken from chapter 17 of the Book Of The Dead (also known as the Book of Going Forth by Day), a section known for its transformation spells. Such spells allowed the deceased to take the form of their wishes as they passed through the underworld to meet Osiris, who would then be asked to give them powers to take a new form. The dead might ask to become a hawk, a lotus, a heron, the crocodile, the Bennu bird or Ptah, for example. Each spell seeks a gift to help their journey. 'The Crocodile', for instance, allows the dead's soul power to become 'the divine crocodile' by inspiring terror and awe when attacking others. Transformation into 'a Heron' requested that the soul earn the gift of knowledge of all incantations so they may take any incarnation they wish at a later time.

Alongside the spells on this box we see various scenes of gods, including Anubis with the body of the deceased Osiris, Isis and her sister Nephthys. The spells tell their story along sides of the object, and the ends of the sarcophagus enjoy the protection of guardian goddesses. Khonsu's mummy evidence suggests he died before his 60th birthday, in 1213 BC.

This magnificent object is of great interest due to the excellent quality of its finish and extremely high standard of hieroglyphic art to be interpreted. Khonsu was the son of a nobleman named Sennedjem. Both were important workers in this purpose-built village near the Valley of the Kings, where those who dug, decorated and held its secrets lived together in a town of some 70 closely packed homes.

Khonsu was a common name in ancient Egypt, being the name of the Egyptian god of the Moon. Here we see a priest of the 25th Dynasty named Ankh-ef-en-Khonsu who also worked in Thebes.

Abu Simbel

The temples of Abu Simbel were built over a 20-year period; construction probably started quite early in the reign of Rameses II, possibly positioned to show Egypt's neighbours where the border stood. The gigantic colossi of Rameses II that adorn the exterior of the main temple are the largest surviving sculptures of a pharaoh. The temples, rooms and sanctuaries within are dedicated to the principal deities of Egypt's great cities and centres of religion – Amun of Thebes, Ptah of Memphis and Ra-Harakhty of Heliopolis. At 34m (110ft) in height, the facade, adorned by four enthroned statues of Rameses II, would surely have simultaneously impressed and awestruck those who wished to challenge Egyptian power. The statues wear the double crown of Upper and Lower Egypt. Inside are halls and sanctuaries dedicated to the union of the temple gods and king. The exterior is decorated with cartouches and hieroglyphs celebrating Rameses II's greatness. There is a frieze with carvings of 22 baboons worshipping the rising sun, and a stele recording that Rameses II married the daughter of a Hittite king, ensuring peace after their wars of earlier years.

The site was built to serve as a lasting monument to the Battle of Kadesh, whose story is told on the facade, where images of fallen enemies are cut into the rock beneath the feet of the pharaoh. The subjugation of the Hittites in this battle took place in 1274 BC, close to the modern border of Lebanon and Syria. The temple carvings show Rameses himself slaying the enemy in what is considered to be the first land war to feature tactical planning, when a pitched battle fought on some 6000 chariots took place. The story of Egypt's victory, in hieroglyphs and paintings, is to be found at Abu Simbel, Luxor Temple, Karnak and other great buildings of Rameses II.

Together with the main temple at Abu Simbel is a smaller temple of Hathor, which was dedicated by Rameses II to his wife Nefertari, who it is believed attended the opening of the

site the year before her death. This monument to his favourite
wife is richly decorated with hieroglyphs and cartouches and
was one of the most astonishing finds of the explorers who
'rediscovered' ancient Egypt. Having been buried under sand
for centuries, the temple was spotted by the Swiss explorer Jean-
Louis Burckhardt in 1813. However, it was Giovanni Belzoni, an
Italian entrepreneur with a British wife, who began clearing the
entrance and excavating in 1817. The temple's interior was first,
and best, described and drawn by Edward William Lane in his
Description of Egypt, published some 10 years later.

*Abu Simbel Temple, featuring colossal statutes of Rameses II, has hieroglyphs that celebrate
the success of the Battle of Kadesh (1274 BC). It was built on a site that marked Egypt's southern border.*

Selected Letters

By the time it fell out of use in the Ptolemaic period, the hieroglyphic script had more than 2000 distinct symbols and countless ways of combining them to express more complex ideas. In addition, hieroglyphs were also used to express an alphabet of 24 individual letters, all of which were consonants. Combinations of these 24 letters into groups of two or three (known as biliteral and triliteral signs) widened the number of words that could be created.

Evidence of the ancient Egyptian language persists in Coptic and echoes of the language are found in later writings. Coptic was a living language when the Rosetta Stone was being deciphered. Selected letters from the hieroglyphic alphabet and their meanings follow in this section.

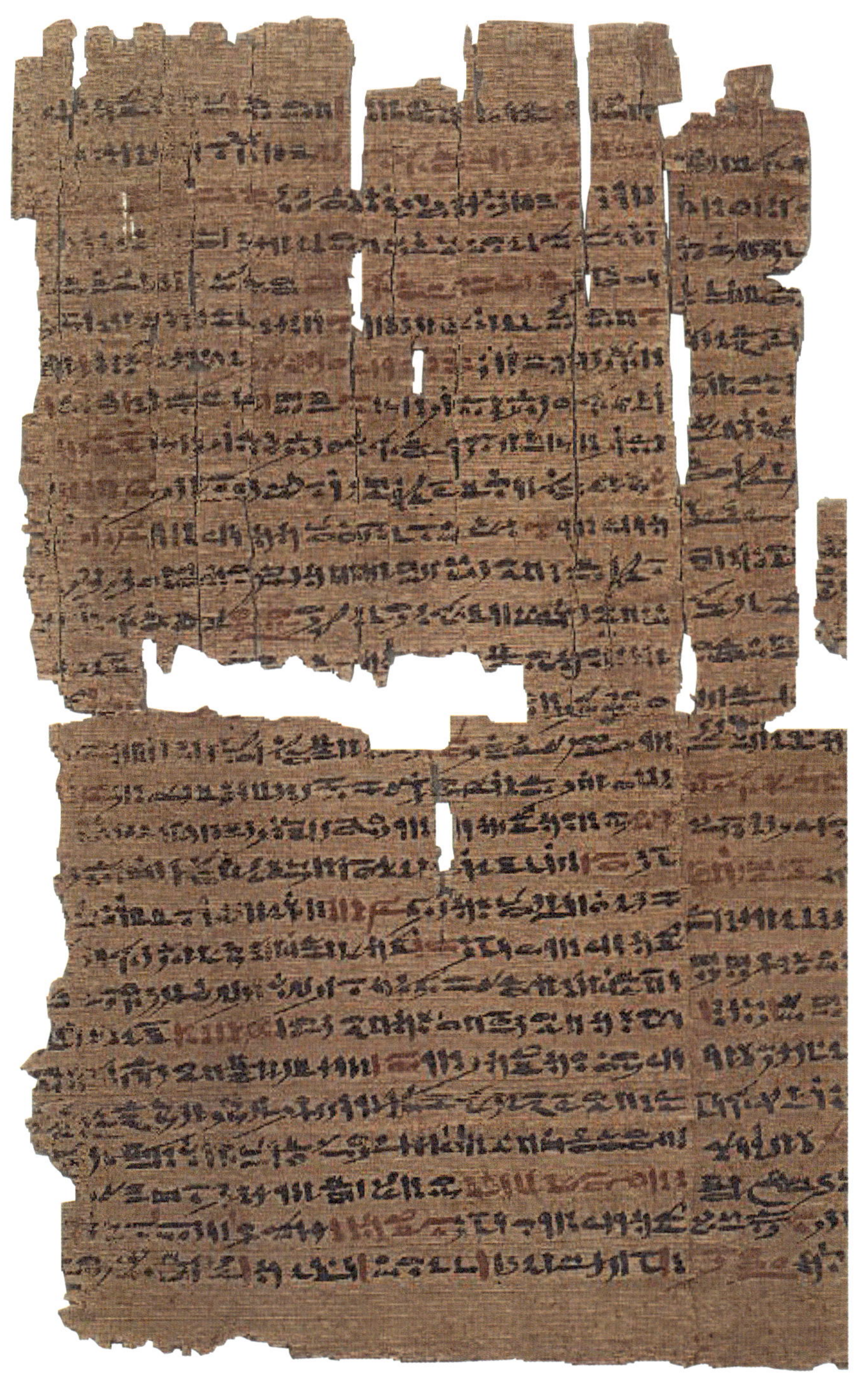

A Brooklyn Museum papyrus that was translated by French Egyptologist Serge Sauneron.
It deals with the topic of venomous snake identification and treatment of snakebites. c. 589–525 BC.

A – Vulture

Symbol:

The vulture appeared in hieroglyphs frequently and represented the letter A in hieroglyphic script and the sound 'ah', as in a vulture's squawk, when spoken. The vulture was a sacred, protected creature with the nickname 'pharaoh's chicken' – indeed, those found killing one would themselves be sentenced to death.

There were several species of vulture in ancient Egypt, with the Egyptian species outline being used most prominently in written language. Its more slender and upright stance helps distinguish it from the larger griffon vulture in other symbols.

Meaning:

The vulture symbol also represented the goddess Nekhbet, protector of Upper Egypt and its rulers. The vulture appeared in many forms in art such as tomb painting, papyrus and sculpture. Although it appears sideways as a hieroglyph, Nekhbet was often shown in painting with her wings spread wide above the pharaoh as protector of the ruler on their throne. The vulture can also be found with wings outspread flying overhead in temples. Such depictions were often representations of Nekhbet. Many queens, including Cleopatra, wore a vulture-shaped headdress.

B – Foot; and D – Hand

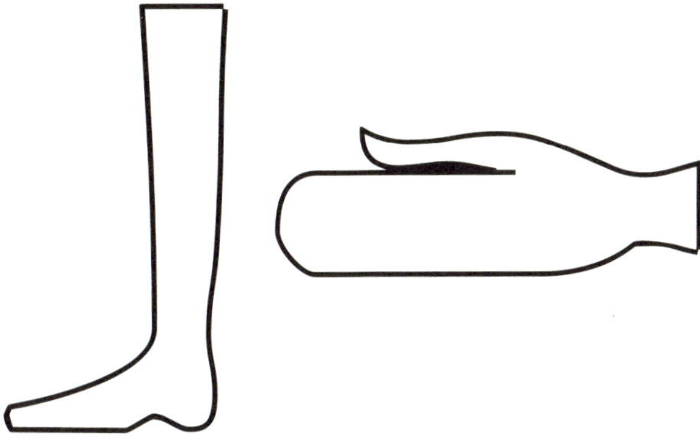

Symbol:

The foot, or more accurately a shortened leg, represents the letter B in the hieroglyphic phonetic alphabet. The symbol for a hand is also a phonogram, representing the letter D. These two symbols are the base for a wide range of other hieroglyphs linked to status, travel and motion, purity and actions of the hand and fist, as well as measurement. Hieroglyphic groups featuring hands are often linked to subduing or repressing enemies and evil.

Meaning:

The foot hieroglyph does not represent movement or walking: these activities are linked to leg symbols. Rather, the foot image is linked to stability and continuity in secular and religious life. When shown above a bowl, its meaning is 'everyone'. In the First Dynasty, the foot hieroglyph was much shorter, with the addition of a leg being seen from the Middle Kingdom onwards. The human hand can be shown from several angles in hieroglyphs. Shown here is the basic representation with the palm facing upwards; it also means 'hand'. Other variants include a clenched fist, meaning grasp, seize or attack, or the palm of a hand, which was a standard measurement on the Egyptian measuring rod.

F – Horned Viper

Symbol:

The horned viper equates to the spoken letter F today. The
viper is extremely venomous and will attack when threatened.
Accordingly there are many protective spells that reflect the
long-held fears of ancient Egyptians. Amulets are commonly
found for use in protecting both the living and the dead from
these snakes during earthly life and beyond. The regenerative
powers of the horned viper gave it special powers in a religion
focused on life and death – its ability to shed one skin and
seem born again was fascinating and many snakes were found
mummified or buried in shrines.

Meaning:

A hieratic papyrus held in the Brooklyn Museum gives detailed
descriptions of the dangers of 38 snakes and other reptiles. It
gives advice on their danger to humans and possible treatments
if one is bitten. Egyptian vipers are given substantial space, with
the horned viper described in detail: '… if the bite is small… [the
patient will have]… fever for nine days but will survive.'

Snakes were associated with the creator god of Egypt, Atum of
Heliopolis. The Hymn of Atum states 'I am the horned snake
whose years are infinite. I lie down dead. I am born daily.'
Snakes were also one of the many sacred animals to Amun,
god of the air.

H – Twisted Flax

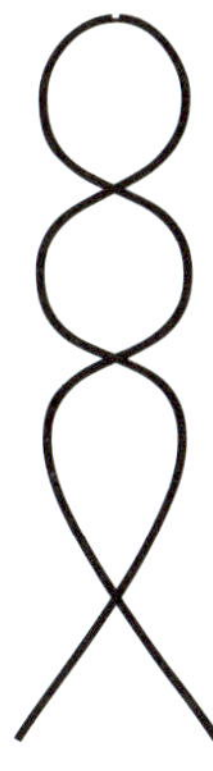

Symbol:
This symbol, a twisted flax that was used to create a lamp wick, represents the letter H in the hieroglyphic alphabet. It's a commonly used symbol, often with the top loop the largest of the three rings in the hieroglyph. In fabric form, it was submerged in animal fats before being lit like oil. Tomb builders in Thebes using this form of lamp relied on production of these and were given them on a daily allowance basis, because they were considered expensive to make. The letter H (pronounced as in 'ha') was a symbol of light and good spirit. This hieroglyph was also a component of the symbol for the deity Ptah.

Meaning:
This symbol holds within it both the agricultural richness of Egypt and the sophistication of the society that was emerging by the Nile. Flax was grown by the Egyptians in fields along the banks of the Nile valley and from it they made linen. Linen is one of the world's earliest fabrics, with remnants found from as early as 5000 BC. The twisted flax was used as a light, like an early form of candle. The light shed from these, stood in a bowl, provided not only illumination to homes and temples but to the many places being worked underground. All of the exquisite tomb paintings and carvings out of reach of daylight were done by firelight, with the long burning twisted flax as a key element.

M – Owl

Symbol:

The owl hieroglyph represents the sound M; two owls (another hieroglyph) is MM. The ancient name for owl had the meaning 'one who laments'. The owl stands alone in hieroglyphs for showing the bird full-face, with only the body in profile, unlike all other creatures. It is generally assumed this reflects the owl's unique ability to turn its head through full circle, as well as its intense gaze from a flat facial structure, which brings character to each bird.

Meaning:

There are indications that the owl was perceived as an unlucky bird by ancient Egyptians, possibly related to its associations with its silent night flights and the eerie calls between owls after dark. They were also associated with mourning and death. No hieroglyphs suggest warmth or reverence, with some showing owls as representing neglectful actions or failure. The main evidence of ancient Egypt's relationship with the bird comes in the mummies of owls, all of which are headless, suggesting an attempt to avoid bad luck in the afterlife by ensuring their destruction. The hieroglyph that represents the expression 'to cut the head off a bird', indeed, features an owl.

Relief plaque with face of an owl hieroglyph, 400–30 BC.

N – Ripple

Symbol:

The source of Egyptian life and centre of its very existence is the Nile river. All life and food drew its sustenance from the wide flowing waters and the vital fertilization of the land following the yearly inundation. Therefore, it is not surprising to find this hieroglyph (and others that include this form) appearing from the earliest times. However, the single ripple is simply a phonogram for the letter N, and when seen alone is not related to water. As a preposition, a single ripple can mean to, for, by, through and because. When used in a group of ripples, the hieroglyph refers to an abundance of water, from lakes and rivers to fast-moving waters or the annual flood.

Meaning:

Ancient Egyptians were understandably absorbed by the rise and fall of the river Nile. The creation god Nu and consort Nunut were the two deities who personified the primeval waters from which the first land appeared and, as such, feature the flood symbol centrally in their hieroglyphic names. In daily Egyptian life, however, it was the god Hapy who was the deity responsible for a successful annual inundation; indeed, the flood itself was referred to as 'the arrival of Hapy'. Because he was a god associated with good harvests and wealth, fertility festivals in his name were a regular part of the Egyptian year, taking place locally as the flood arrived.

T – Loaf of Bread

Symbol:

Bread in the shape of the rising sun is the symbol representing the letter T in the hieroglyphic alphabet. It is the first of eight separate bread symbols in the core hieroglyphic list. These include differing types of bread shape, including bread rolls and sweet bread desserts. The hieroglyphs carry double symbolism beyond being food for the Egyptians, because bread was also a vital offering used to feed the gods and the deceased. When it is shown as a triangle, as here, it represents words and phrases linked to the act of giving.

Meaning:

Bread was a basic dietary item in ancient Egypt. Bread and beer, made from grain, were consumed with almost every meal. Egypt relied heavily on its grain harvest and storage. Farming occupied almost every working family, at all stages of life. The main crops were emmer, which had arrived from Syria thousands of years earlier, barley and flax. Bread's central role means it features in many texts from ancient Egypt, with multiple shapes of loaf included. A symbol showing the conical loaf, held in the hand, has the meaning 'to give'. Egyptian art depicts all stages of bread making, from detailed wooden and clay models of Egyptians and their farm animals threshing and crushing grain to baking ovens and feasts. In addition to bread, barley was used extensively for beer making.

Z or S – Door Bolt and Folded Cloth

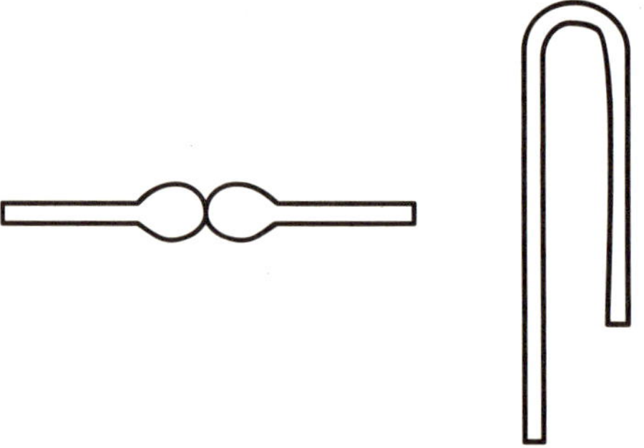

Symbol:

These two symbols both represent the letter S in the hieroglyphic alphabet (being the horizontal and vertical versions). The door bolt shown accurately mirrors examples of bolts that survived because of their high quality. These were to secure the doors of temples and chapels that held statues of gods. The folded cloth is an image linked to security and, more particularly, good health and long life.

Meaning:

Doors in ancient Egypt were a symbol (in private life) of wealth and success. The wealthy employed a door-keeper to guard the premises, a role still commonly seen in Egypt, overseeing the entrance to a villa or an apartment block. Doors to public and religious buildings had a double door, hence the need for a bolt. The closing and opening of these sacred spaces signalled times for important daily rituals. A temple, for instance, may have several small chapels containing statues of gods, each of which were closed after dark and secured with a three-ring bolt structure that would still be familiar today.

The folded cloth hieroglyph can be seen in groups of symbols relating to the wellbeing of the pharaoh and has also been traditionally associated with the portrayal of rank or office.

Stele of Roma the door-keeper dedicated to the goddess Astarte, 18th Dynasty,
New Kingdom, c. 1400–1365 BC.

Picture Credits

Alamy: 11 (Ian Dagnall), 18 (Album), 19 (Prisma Archivo), 20 (Album), 51 (Hemis), 59 (Seth Lazar), 61 (BasPhoto), 69 (agefotostock), 73 (Album), 103 (North Wind Picture Archives), 111 (Mike P Shepherd), 113 (BasPhoto), 123 (travelpixs), 133 (Granger Historical Picture Archive), 139 (Terence Waeland)

Brooklyn Museum, New York: 149

Dreamstime: 23 (Krzyssagit), 27 (Basphoto), 41 (Tomwyness), 47 (Wirestock), 55 (Neilneil), 67 (Icon72), 71 (Mfcaulliez), 87 (Svetlaili), 147 (Davemusic8)

Getty Images: 13 (Photo Josse/Leemage), 15 (Print Collector), 17 (Hanis), 37 (De Agostini/S Vannini), 75 (Werner Forman), 83 (De Agostini/S Vannini), 91 (De Agostini), 95 (Barney Burstein), 117 (Gian Berto Vanni), 119 (Werner Forman), 121 (Paul Biris), 129 (Culture Club), 135 (Amir Makar), 141 (duncan1890), 143 (De Agostini/G Dagli Orti), 145 (De Agostini/W Buss), 159 (Universal Images Group)

Licensed under the Creative Commons Attribution 4.0 International licence: 85 (Osama Shukir Muhammed Amin FRCP(Glasg))

Metropolitan Museum of Art, New York: 21, 33, 77, 79, 81, 99, 109, 125, 131, 155

Public Domain: 7, 9, 89, 137

Shutterstock: 3 (Fedor Selivanov), 57 (Sculpies), 65 (Pakhnyushchy), 93 (bumihills), 105 (MindStorm)

All hieroglyph illustrations are by Kit Soccer via Shutterstock, except for pages 50 (Eroshka/Shutterstock), 52 (Sidhe/Shutterstock), 66 (Peter Hermes Furian/Dreamstime), 98 (Patrick Mulrey) and 150 (Isaac Zakar/Shutterstock)

Background images by Alvaro Cabrera Jimenez via Shutterstock